Amazing Grace
Overcoming Race

Larry D. Oney

AMAZING GRACE OVERCOMING RACE
Written by Larry D. Oney
Copyright © 2012 by Larry D. Oney
Printed in the United States

ISBN: 1478117567
ISBN-13: 978-1478117568

Lovingly dedicated to Andi:

My most cherished friend

CONTENTS

Letter to the Reader   i

1   Chapter One   1

2   Chapter Two   5

3   Chapter Three   9

4   Chapter Four   13

5   Chapter Five   17

6   Chapter Six   21

7   Chapter Seven   23

8   Chapter Eight   27

9   Chapter Nine   31

10   Chapter Ten   35

11   Chapter Eleven   39

12   Chapter Twelve   43

13   Chapter Thirteen   47

14   Chapter Fourteen   51

15   Chapter Fifteen   55

16   Chapter Sixteen   59

17   Chapter Seventeen   63

18   Chapter Eighteen   67

19   Chapter Nineteen   71

20   Chapter Twenty   75

21   Chapter Twenty-One   81

22   Chapter Twenty-Two   85

23   Chapter Twenty-Three   89

24   Chapter Twenty-Four   93

25   Chapter Twenty-Five   97

26   Chapter Twenty-Six   101

27   Chapter Twenty-Seven   105

28   Chapter Twenty-Eight   109

29   Chapter Twenty-Nine   115

30   Chapter Thirty   119

31   Chapter Thirty-One   125

32   Chapter Thirty-Two   131

33   Chapter Thirty-Three   137

34   Chapter Thirty-Four   141

35   Chapter Thirty-Five   147

36   Chapter Thirty-Six   153

37   Chapter Thirty-Seven   157

38   Chapter Thirty-Eight   163

39   Chapter Thirty-Nine   167

40   Chapter Forty   171

41   Chapter Forty-One   175

42   Chapter Forty-Two   179

43   Chapter Forty-Three   183

LETTER TO THE READER

Dear Reader,

I set out to tell the story of the journey of my faith until this point with the hope that I could lift up the name of the Lord and His amazing grace, as well as to give a different perspective and insight on the power of God's love and its ability to overcome no matter what circumstances we are currently in or have experienced. God's amazing grace is so expansive that it is like a great tree with room under its branches for all of His children.

In this book you will hear about the realities of injustice, poverty, struggle, and about the power of God's triumphant love and His amazing grace that He gives us on the journey of our lives up to the house of the Father. Sometimes this outpouring of God's grace is imperceptible to us, but nonetheless the weight of His glory still presses in on us.

Larry

CHAPTER ONE
LIVING IN EGYPT

LARRY'S STORY:

I was seven years old when my entire life changed forever. During the early 1960s, on a cool bright morning, I stuffed my lanky frame onto the open windowsill of our tiny house and pulled one leg up to my chin. Pants with holes in them exposed freshly scabbed knees while my dirt-crusted bare foot dangled in the slight breeze. I perched quietly, studying my dad and the white landowner standing in our yard.

I was rigid with curiosity because the landowner had actually gotten out of his truck. No landowner in the Louisiana Delta would actually take the effort to get out of his truck just to come and speak to a black sharecropper unless something serious or important was happening. They stood near the electric water pump that had been put in only days earlier. The dirt collected around the new installation was still fresh on the ground.

I watched the white man rest his hands on his hips. He appeared to be frustrated or annoyed about something. I saw his head tilt. He pushed his grey, banded hat to one side. His clean white shirt reflected against the bright sun, making me squint. He was not talking ugly to my dad, but he was clearly letting him know what he expected and what he wanted.

Towering over the white landowner, my dad seemed to stand as tall as the sky. His powerful hands were impressive. I knew if he wanted to, he could snap a man in half. He had plenty of chances, though he never dared. One false move in front of a white man would have meant his life. Dad was tall, at least 6'4", but there was no question as to who was in charge and who held the power during this exchange.

My dad, known as Bubba, held a subservient, humble posture in front of the property-owner. Despite the immense difference in their size, their mannerisms told the story without words. However, words were spoken. From my window seat, I heard them. Those words etched themselves into my brain and created a dramatic influence on the rest of my life.

The white man spoke sternly, "Bubba, don't you let Bea take these boys away from here. I've been good to ya'll." (Bea was my mother.) Pointing to the water pump, his clean shirt glinted against the sun. The white man heartlessly reminded my dad about some basic repairs done to the house to keep the wind from shooting through the bottom of the floor in the wintertime. It was clear that he did not want us boys taken off the land, as the eight boys were a significant labor source.

The landowner knew that my mom wanted to move away from the plantation. The landowner held the power and dictated to my dad not to let us leave. My dad could only say, "Yessa'." Dad did not have the power to resist the demands of the landowner, but my mom had other ideas.

Looking back, I realize that race, and the power it allowed one group of people over another, had forcefully swept into my awareness. The fear, anxiety, and hatred would only be washed away many years later when God's amazing grace would help me to overcome race. (Not that any of us ever completely overcomes the pain and the indignity of one race asserting itself over another race, but each of us can make a decision with God's grace to forgive those that have hurt us in matters of race.)

My father, Clifton Oney, was a survivor and he knew his place. My dad grew up on the dicey edge of brutality, when a white man could legally beat a black man down to the ground for little or no reason. I am sure my dad's size caused him to know this misery first-hand. Being a large man made him a target of sorts. Any slight movement, or the smallest amount of defiance, could bring him harm, or even death.

"Stop judging by appearances, but judge justly."

—John 7:24, NABRE

GOD'S GRACE:

Sometimes when a painful or traumatic event happens, people can become guarded and wary of others. The Enemy wants a person to feel alone and like he cannot escape whatever trauma he is enduring. God, on the other hand, desires for people to know that they are not alone. God provides the Armor of God (see Ephesians 6:11 below). With God's armor, we are able to withstand the arrows of the Enemy. The taunts that our enemies try to hurl at us like arrows no longer hurt because we can now see that they are in pain and do not know the Truth. We can begin to feel empathy for our enemies and pray for them and their healing. God's grace allows us to feel compassion for others—even those who would hurt us.

"Put on the armor of God so that you may be able to stand firm against the tactics of the devil."
—Ephesians 6:11, NABRE

CHAPTER TWO
PARENTS

LARRY'S STORY:

My mother's name was Beatrice Allen and she had thirteen children with my father, Clifton Oney; however, two children died at birth. My parents were never married. All of my brothers and sisters have the last name of Allen. I am the only child with my father's last name, even though we all have the same father and mother.

My mother was not well after having me so my dad had to go and register me with the parish (county) in order for her to get medical care. My father only had a third grade education, so he could sign his name and that was all. He did not understand that a child born to an unwed mother got the last name of the mother. Therefore, I got his last name—Oney. I have had to explain this all my life, sometimes with embarrassment.

When I reached the eighth grade, I had my heart set on playing sports, especially basketball. The school demanded a copy of my birth certificate. I had been using my mother's last name (Allen) until the school officials found out what was actually on my birth certificate. For the first time in my life, I had to use my real last name, Oney.

"For through faith you are all children of God in Christ Jesus."
—Galatians 3:26, NABRE

GOD'S GRACE:

Our name represents who we are and often gives us a sense of self. Children are often taught to "live up to your name," or "be proud of your name." Names are important, but we should always remember that we are children of God. God created us to have a relationship with Him. To God, we are more than our earthly name. Notice that in the Bible, God changes the name of a person to reflect who they really are in His eyes:

Abram became Abraham (See Genesis 17:5)
Simon became Peter (See Matthew 16:18)

We must begin to see ourselves as God sees us. God loves us. God sees us as we truly are. We look in the mirror and see all of our "flaws." Yet, when God looks at us, He sees our hearts. Yes, God does see the physical parts of us, but He created us in His own image—to God, we are all beautiful and unique. God is not color blind—God loves color and He chose to create each of us as beautiful human beings. To God, each human is a work of art and He is the artist.

LARRY D. ONEY

CHAPTER THREE
FAMILY

LARRY'S STORY:

The leader of the family, indisputably, was my oldest brother A.C., and then my next older brother, Cliff. After that, it would be George. Both George and Cliff are ordained ministers today; one is a Pentecostal and the other is a Baptist Minister.

Our family was a loving family, but my father was somewhat removed. I did not really understand why my dad was gone so much and I was angry with him for not being present enough during my childhood.

My dad was a very hard worker and well known on the plantation. Even though he was a tractor driver, a coveted role on the plantation, he made my mom starch and iron his pants every day. She used the old type of starch that she actually had to mix before ironing. Dad always went to work looking crisp and always returned home dirty. He wore a cap on the top of his head and for some reason he was very contentious about how he looked.

I do not remember my parents having much fun. I remember the tension about the lack of money and not having enough to eat. I wish I could say that my parents were nurturing, but I never felt like I was nurtured—certainly not by my father, and not very much by my mother. In fact, I cannot ever remember really being held very often by my mother. Our family was just too large and there was little time for anything but work.

Toward the end of her life, before my mom died, we were very close and we spoke, not so much as mother and son, but as two people on a spiritual path. She was the matriarch and the strength of our family. I knew that she loved me. She was a prayerful woman, but I knew that there was a lot of pain in her life.

My mom was short in stature but tall in wisdom. She was a beautiful woman, one-quarter Cherokee Indian with a full head of coarse black hair. She was very gracious. I guess everybody thinks that their mom is beautiful, and I am no exception. Even though she only had a fifth grade education, she was very smart.

My brothers James and Bobby were the ones I looked up to. They were closest to me in age. It seemed like they could do almost anything. I often felt inconsequential as a young child because there were so many of us. It seemed like I was never able to do what the older kids were doing. One time in particular, I remember standing on the porch watching my older brother climb into his old, blue car.

Going for a ride, several others stuffed themselves into the vehicle until the car was full. I had to stay behind. I wanted to go too, but they all laughed and said I was too young.

> "He found them in a wilderness,
> a wasteland of howling desert.
> He shielded them, cared for them,
> guarded them as the apple of his eye."
> —Deuteronomy 32:10, NABRE

GOD'S GRACE:

Whether we grow up in a loving home with both parents or are raised by someone other than a parent, God wants everyone to come to Him. As we grow in our faith, God becomes our true Father—a parent who loves us and will not abandon us. We are truly children of God. (See Ephesians 1:3-8; 2 Corinthians 6:17-18; 1 John 3:1; and Romans 8:17.)

As children of God, we are free to go to Him at any time and speak with Him about our life, our needs, and our wants, while knowing that God wants to give us good things as a loving Father would. God has a good future planned for us and He is waiting for us to come to Him and discuss it with Him. As children of God, we can find our hope and our freedom.

"See what love the Father has bestowed on us that we may be called the children of God. Yet so we are. The reason the world does not know us is that it did not know him."
—1 John 3:1, NABRE

CHAPTER FOUR
LIFE

LARRY'S STORY:

As sharecroppers, the landowners dominated us. They controlled the amount of food available, the hours we worked, and where we lived. Though I had a home in rural northern Louisiana, it was as if we were living in Egypt. The undeniable, unavoidable chains of bondage held me, my family, and all the black folk around us. It felt as though we were simply manacled puppets and the white landowners pulled the strings, *those invisible chains*, as they pleased. There was no regard for age or sex. Men and women, young and old, were manipulated within the carefully crafted structure of the sharecropper economy.

The place where my family resided was called Holly Brook Plantation, which I now refer to as Egypt. For black people, sharecropping was the way of life in the Deep South during the early

1960s. The physical shackles of subjugation had long since been removed from my ancestors; however, the emotional and psychological bondage of enslavement was still clearly present. All of us who worked the land at Holly Brook found ourselves swallowed up by racism, intimidation, and hopelessness.

We lived down a long road from the main highway. Way Way Lane was a very dusty, hard gravel road. You could see someone coming from a long way off. A cloud of grit flared with each approaching vehicle. Our house was nothing more than a shack with tarpaper on the outside. The little structure held my parents, Clifton and Beatrice, as well as eight boys and three girls. I was the seventh born out of eleven.

Our small kitchen had one large table that we all had to squeeze around. We did not eat with our parents. Mom served Dad and then she usually ate after him, but not with us. Dad always ate first. My father got the best of everything. Children would not dare eat before the father. That's just how it was in my family and in most of the black families on the plantation. Children rarely spoke in the presence of adults. We were not allowed to speak to adults on any casual terms.

When it was time to eat, everybody knew it and we did not have to be called twice. If someone did not eat quickly enough the older kids would eat whatever was on that person's plate. You came hungry and you ate as fast as you could. There was no forcing anybody to eat their leftovers. In our house, there was no such thing as leftovers. My brother James and I used to laugh about that as we grew up. Watching television shows about families forced to eat leftovers, or making sure that you ate everything on your plate was unheard of in our house. I was at least thirty years old before I learned to slow down and eat at a normal pace.

The younger children shared a room, and the older children shared a room. Our bedrooms were walled with thin partitions. The first time we had some paint on the walls, it was a loud blue. We all slept crammed at both ends of the bed, toward the head and toward the foot. Sleeping in the summer heat was almost impossible but in the winter, we were glad for the extra body heat. The beds were very crowded. Our beds consisted of the sack material that was used for hauling cotton. The sacks were sewn together and cotton from the fields was stuffed inside, creating a mattress. Every morning we had to toss the cotton around inside the mattress to freshen it up. It was not a pretty sight. We always slept with some kind of bugs in the bed, flakes of dried earth from the fields, and God only knows what else. If there was any bed-wetting or anything like that, the sack-filled cotton bedding was fluffed up and turned over. My mom was too busy after working in the fields, feeding eleven kids, and taking care of a husband, to do any more than she did. Some evenings we had a bath and others we went to bed dirty.

"…though I sit in darkness, the LORD is my light."
—Micah 7:8c, NABRE

GOD'S GRACE:

Have you ever felt dominated or oppressed? Being controlled by someone else, even in a game, can be a frightening experience. As we begin to know Jesus, we begin to realize that we are free. Some people associate Jesus with more rules; yet, the Truth is that with Jesus there is true freedom—we are free to be healed of our past, we are free to believe in a better future for ourselves and our families, and we are free to become the person that we were meant to be as God created us to be before sin.

This may not be an overnight process, but Jesus begins to heal us from our pain and disappointments from the moment that we come to Him. Jesus is always gentle and He heals us at our own pace. Some issues may take more time to heal because they are so traumatic or because they have been a part of our lives for so long. Jesus does not rush us in the healing process—He understands that some things take time to truly heal and Jesus wants to make sure that we are healed and that we find true freedom in Christ.

CHAPTER FIVE
WATER

LARRY'S STORY:

Our house was owned by the plantation owner. Sharecroppers rarely owned any of the land or houses and we were no different. There was no indoor plumbing at all. Our house was the same as most, except we had the small electric pump in the yard instead of the regular hand-crank pump the other families had to use. Our electric pump was an enticement because we provided so many laborers for the field.

For most of the years that we stayed at that house, I remember having to take a little water and put it into the hand-crank pump to get the water moving from under the ground. It seemed that we were constantly carrying water from the pump to the house to wash dishes and clean things. It was a continual, non-stop process. Going out to use the bathroom after dark was a real adventure. If I couldn't wait for daylight, I ran as fast as I could, ignored the sounds around me in the blackness of night, and ran back to the house. Even though the electric pump was not anything fancy and was still outside, it was a big help. Most of the other black families did not have this luxury. Whenever I saw the pump, it was a sore reminder of the landowner's domination, of his attempt to keep my father and us boys on the land.

The laundry was done on a hand-cranked machine and then hung on the clothesline. Hanging clothes out on the clothesline was the source of many battles between my sister and me. Taking a bath was also interesting, to say the least. In the small washtub, called a foot-tub, my parents were the only ones that had fresh, hot water. Children had to bathe in the water that somebody already used, and *maybe* on the third or fourth time, the water would be changed.

Bath water was room temperature and not heated since there was no way to easily heat water, except from the stove. That was an indulgence generally held for my parents. I hate to say it, but we did not bathe every day. That was just an unpleasant fact for our large family. Food and money were more important than bathing.

"…but whoever drinks the water I shall give will never thirst; the water I shall give will become in him a spring of water welling up to eternal life."
—John 4:14, NABRE

GOD'S GRACE:

For some, feeling clean and feeling worthy go hand-in-hand. If we are newly showered and dressed nicely, we have more self-confidence and feel more in control of a situation. The opposite can also be true—if we are not physically clean then we can feel ashamed or somehow less than others. God sees our hearts. God sees what is on the inside of a person.

> "I will sprinkle clean water over you to make you clean; from all your impurities and from all your idols I will cleanse you."
> —Ezekiel 36:25, NABRE

LARRY D. ONEY

CHAPTER SIX
FLYING

LARRY'S STORY:

I loved jumping off the porch. It was the closest thing to flying. When Momma made me sweep the porch, I usually found myself swept up with the idea of flying and not cleaning. I always tried to see if I could jump further than the day before. Like other children, I was often looking for things to do when I wasn't working in the fields.

There was a shed where my dad kept his black Chevy Impala. He kept his cars spotless and inside the shed. Once, I climbed up on the tall shed. It seemed like I was several stories up and scared to death. When I jumped off, I felt like I was in the air forever. I landed shaken, but with no broken bones. I never went up on that shed again. That ended my obsession with flight.

> "Who are these that fly along like a cloud,
> Like doves to their cotes."
> —Isaiah 60:8, NABRE

GOD'S GRACE:

This world bombards people with escapism opportunities. Escaping through temporary measures is never a good solution. Asking Jesus to help us to see good solutions and to help us to have the strength to make those positive changes is more productive than trying to "escape." It is possible to make changes in our lives. We may not know the solution ourselves, but God does know. For God, all things are possible. (See Mark 10:27; Matthew 19:26; Mark 14:36; and Luke 18:27.) This was such an important teaching that it appears multiple times in the Gospels. We don't have to depend only on our own abilities; rather, we can depend on God.

Jesus looked at them and said, "For human beings it is impossible,
but not for God. All things are possible for God."
—Mark 10:27, NABRE

CHAPTER SEVEN
GARDEN

LARRY'S STORY:

Every house on the plantation had a garden. Sharecropper families would not have been able to make it through the winters without one. Our garden played a key role in my family's winter survival as well. My mother canned everything she could from that garden. We ate mostly canned vegetables during the cold months. In our little garden, we grew corn, tomatoes, sweet potatoes, butter beans, snap beans, and all sorts of vegetables. *I have eaten my share of vegetables to last me a lifetime!*

During the season when we waited for our vegetables to grow, we could always get turnip greens. They seemed to spring up continuously. There were plenty of wild mustard greens alongside the roads. They grew everywhere. I was not so sure those mustard greens were safe for us to eat. They grew at the edge of the cotton and soybean fields that were tainted by poisonous fertilizing chemicals saturating the ground. Even so, we ate them and we still lived.

My brothers and I supplemented the winter stockpile by seining small fish and freezing them. Cleaning, gutting, and freezing the fish was a messy job but we could not rely on the garden alone. It was nice to have something besides vegetables. Everybody had chores like feeding the few cows, pigs, and goats that we owned. In the wintertime, we had to collect wood and sticks, cut the wood, and haul it inside for the stove. Everybody had something to do. We also got "commodity food," which was supplemental food the government gave to poor families. We were very, very happy to get that food.

"Fear not, for I am with you."
—Isaiah 43:5, NABRE

GOD'S GRACE:

God provides for His people. When we turn to God and seek Him, God pours out His blessings upon us. As we begin to believe in God and believe God, our trust and faith will grow. With faith and trust, we learn to depend on God, to seek God and tell Him when we have needs and God, in His mercy, will provide for us. God's provision may not come in the way we want it to or in the way we expect, but God does provide.

"Then the Lord said to Moses: I am going to rain down bread from heaven for you."
—Exodus 16:4a, NABRE

LARRY D. ONEY

CHAPTER EIGHT
TREATS AND EATS

LARRY'S STORY:

On the Plantation, almost every Sunday we would go visit Aunt Ma. She was a great and gentle woman who sold little boxes of candy. People would walk a mile or two just to buy her five-cent or ten-cent candy. She never allowed us to buy her candy. She knew we did not have any money for luxuries like candy. However, before we left her house, Aunt Ma would always make sure that all of us got a three-colored piece of flat candy for free. Whenever we went to visit anyone, we were told that we should never ask for anything to eat. If we were offered food, we had to turn it down. Aunt Ma never asked if we were hungry; she would just give us something to eat. I have fond memories of her and the nice smile on her face.

Almost every day at home, I knew what we were going to eat. Meals were usually a simple pan of flatbread and beans. We had white beans, butter beans, or some other kind of beans. During the summer, we ate more vegetables than I care to remember. The only time that we got fruit was when my cousins came to visit us from the New Orleans area. Whenever they came, they brought us oranges and apples. It was like manna from heaven. We never had the ability to purchase our own fruit from the grocery store. We couldn't afford to waste money on extras. Fruit was considered a treat.

There was scarcely enough food to make it through the colder months. One winter, my dad took his rifle and set out to kill some black birds for food. It was extremely cold and we literally had nothing to eat. It did not matter that there was so little meat on those black bird's bones. Momma managed to make up a pot of black bird stew and we were grateful to have it.

One time my mother allowed me to go with her and my dad to the grocery store. There was a lady working behind the counter cutting sandwiches into nice, perfect little squares. I did not dare ask for anything but I did make several passes in front of her, attempting to get her attention. I wanted to try that delicious looking sandwich she had created. It was prepared with an incredible, yellow creamy substance. For the first time in my life, I had a store-bought sandwich with mustard on it. I had never tasted mustard before and it was the most amazing thing!

He continued: "Go, eat rich foods and drink sweet drinks, and allot portions to those who had nothing prepared; for today is holy to our LORD. Do not be saddened this day, for rejoicing in the LORD is your strength!"
—Nehemiah 8:10, NABRE

GOD'S GRACE:

God wants the best for us. When Jesus was tempted in the wilderness, the first temptation dealt with food because He was hungry. Jesus had not eaten for 40 days. Jesus knew hunger. Yet Jesus pointed out that man does not live by bread alone, but by the Word of God. God wants to provide for all of our needs, not just our physical needs, but for our spiritual needs as well.

> Filled with the holy Spirit, Jesus returned from the Jordan and was led by the Spirit into the desert for forty days, to be tempted by the devil. He ate nothing during those days, and when they were over he was hungry. The devil said to him, "If you are the Son of God, command this stone to become bread." Jesus answered him, "It is written, 'One does not live by bread alone.'" —Luke 4:1-4, NABRE

LARRY D. ONEY

CHAPTER NINE
SCHOOL

LARRY'S STORY:

Clothes were mostly hand-me-downs from child to child, as we rarely had clothes that were new. One of the most humiliating times in Holly Brook was wearing shoes stuffed with paper because they had holes in them. Even worse than that, was the lack of a belt. When I went to school, I had to put a stick in my pants that twisted over loop-to-loop. I had to either use a stick, or let my pants fall down.

There was a boy named Henry Lee who always liked to wrestle at recess. I did not like wrestling with him because I thought somebody would see the stick in my pants. As a result, I would have to find the perfect little stick, one that would not poke or hurt me, but would keep my pants up. Having paper in my shoes and a stick in my pants was not fun.

Nevertheless, I really liked going to school. I knew there was going to be food there. There was no such thing as "free lunch" when I was in school. Ms. Clay, a kind and wonderful woman, was one of my teachers. If someone could not afford the ten-cent lunch, she would speak to the people in the cafeteria ahead of time, telling them to put some of her food on this person or that person's plate. In doing so, nobody would know when someone could not afford lunch. Ms. Clay did so much for me during that time. She was a woman of mercy, sharing her food while guarding the dignity of young poor people, including me.

I knew we were poor because of a young friend that we went to school with whose name was Kenneth. He always had nice clothes, he was very confident, and he got a haircut every month. We only got haircuts every six months. He always looked fresh and wore good shoes. He could buy a soda anytime he wanted to. I thought Kenneth was rich!

All there was for black kids to look forward to after graduating high school was working the fields by either chopping cotton or getting on a tractor to spread the poison and turn over the dirt. Driving a tractor meant getting away from the sharp boughs, not hunching and stooping all day. It was all we could hope for. Elevation in this type of bondage would only mean that one would be an overseer of the people. Instead of handling poison or turning dirt, we could only look forward to becoming a paymaster to pay the nickels and dimes, or the two cents a pound, to the cotton pickers during the summer months.

"When you call me, and come and pray to me, I will listen to you. When you look for me, you will find me. Yes, when you seek me with all your heart, I will let you find me…and I will change your lot."
—Jeremiah 29:12-14a, NABRE

GOD'S GRACE:

Every person is priceless to God, no matter how much money we have or what kind of clothes we may wear. We are precious to God. When God looks at us, He does not see our clothes; He sees that we are a princes or princesses of the Kingdom of God. There is no higher "ranking" that we can achieve. As an heir in the Kingdom, we know that we are clothed by God. (See Galatians 3:26-27 and Isaiah 61:10-11.)

For through faith you are all children of God in Christ Jesus. For all of you who were baptized into Christ have clothed yourselves with Christ.
—Galatians 3:26-27, NABRE

CHAPTER TEN
WORKING THE FIELDS

LARRY'S STORY:

My life as a youngster seemed primarily centered on struggling to have enough to eat and long hours of hard work. It did not matter if you were a boy or girl. When you reached age seven, you went to the fields. I was anxious about working at such a young age because I did not know what was expected of me. I had never picked or chopped cotton before.

Every morning during the chopping season, the driver would pick us up on the truck while it was still dark so we could be at the field right at the break of day. We could not start chopping the cotton before daylight. In the dark, the men and older boys would be sharpening the hoes. I did not like that sound of steel on steel because it created a tension in my body from the grating sound. It made me anxious. Hoes were then tossed upside-down into a box situated at the back of the truck, and they rattled around in the blackness.

The driver would already have the ice for the community water bucket. It was pitch dark but I could hear the sound of the block of ice hitting the bucket. Grasshoppers, crickets, and frogs echoed against the noise. The darkness held millions of insects that sounded like an orchestra of clicking, chirping, and whistling.

Everybody stepped up on the truck, and stepped down—old women, young women, young people. Everybody was quiet in the morning. It was eerie to be on the back of the truck going to the field as a child. You do not know where you are going. You do not know how far you are going. You were just plain scared! The first couple of days that I went out were the scariest. I had no idea where I was; everything seemed huge. I was with adults that I had not been around before. Nobody was paying attention to me; I was on my own. I learned how to chop the cotton by doing it.

Picking the cotton was an entirely different process than chopping. To get the cotton off the stalks and into the sack was new to me. No one stopped and taught me. I just figured it out as I went. I learned to pick the cotton, put it in the sack, and drag it to the paymaster staging area, which was stationed somewhere at the end of one of the rows. Everybody was in the field. The women would have rags around their heads and the men mostly wore hats. Even in the summer, we all wore long sleeves because the sharp cotton boughs would slice into our skin and the chemicals would get on our arms. Many of us had rashes and medical problems from constantly being around the chemicals.

Even though I was a child, no one stopped to help me when the razor-sharp boughs cut my tender skin. Early on, as I pulled the puffy cotton from their sharp, pointy cradles, I wished for a pile of that fluff to fall onto and rest. In the springtime, the weather was a little bit cooler, but in the summer, it was very humid and hot. We all drank water from a common dipper. Sometimes they had horses in the field for the weaker people who could pick large sacks, but could not always drag that weight to the staging area.

Picking cotton was just the same as chopping it; we got out there as early as you could to avoid the stifling heat in the middle of the day. You had to get up as much momentum as possible before the heat was too much. Everybody sweated like crazy. I remember even the old people sweated. Salty sweat burned in the deep wounds from the cotton boughs and taught me to pick carefully. Some older women were particularly good at managing huge sacks of cotton. They would strap the sack around their shoulders and pull it along, bending and stooping as they hauled their sack toward the horses.

While working, I sometimes dreamed of playing. We played with the old tires from tractors that were in the fields. Our swimming pool was the runoff ditch at the end of the fields where the poisonous chemicals gathered in odd-looking colors. It was a dangerous pastime, but our only escape from the heat and the bitterness we felt toward the white landowners.

> "For the LORD will be your light forever,
> And the days of your grieving will be over."
> —Isaiah 60:20, NABRE

GOD'S GRACE:

When we are in a difficult situation, it is easy to become bitter with the situation or with a person. It is important to deal with our bitterness right away through prayer. Prayer is an essential part of a Christian's spiritual life. Communicating with God is an important way to develop our relationship with Him.

Bitterness can cut off our view of God or make us feel alienated from God if we let the bitterness grow. Questions like, *"Where is God when I need Him?"* can begin to invade our thinking. Bitterness can also cause a person to feel cut off from friends, family, or the church. This is what the enemy wants—Satan wants us to feel cut off and alone, full of bitterness and anger.

Learning to forgive the difficult circumstances that we have lived through can be very healing. With Jesus' help, the bitterness and disappointment that we may have suffered doesn't have to have a strangle hold on us for the rest of our lives—we can be set free.

> Jesus answered them, "Amen, amen, I say to you, everyone who commits sin is a slave of sin. A slave does not remain in a household forever, but a son always remains. So if a son frees you, then you will truly be free." —John 8:34-36, NABRE

CHAPTER ELEVEN
WORK AND PLAY

LARRY'S STORY:

The rows of soybeans and cotton appeared to go on forever. To my young eyes, those rows looked like they were miles and miles long. I remember thinking that there was no way that I would ever finish one row. I still do not know how I did. Today, I can certainly understand how the Israelites felt down in Egypt. Their work seemed to have no end. Our work seemed to have no end in sight either.

I had to pick a lot of cotton. Looking at the big trailer filled with a white, fluffy bounty was intimidating. At age seven, I could not empty my own sack. I had to get somebody else to empty it for me. If I picked fifty pounds, I would get one dollar. The problem with getting one dollar at the end of the day was that I actually ended up with around sixty cents for all of my work.

I had no food to bring to the field with me so I bought lunch from people who sold food in the fields. A person could buy a soft drink and a sandwich, or a piece of meat and some bread, and spend between twenty-five and forty cents. Some of the older guys would make as much as four or five, maybe even six dollars a day picking cotton, but that would mean they would pick two to three hundred pounds of cotton. It was an astonishing feat! I was always impressed with how they could get all that cotton in those long sacks and drag it to the weigh station.

I did not like chopping the cotton. I did not like having constant painful cuts and scabs. I did not like being poor. I did not like having paper in my shoes or wearing my brother's shoes that were too big. I did not like having a stick in my pants. I couldn't complain or protest. Everyone was in the same boat.

I also could not understand why the planes would spray poisonous chemicals right on top of us as we were working in the fields. There was a total disregard for the workers: my brothers, sisters, relatives, and myself. It was depressing. I hated every minute of it.

However, the depression would subside late in the day when we would get to roll tires with my cousins. They lived about a quarter mile away. We played what we would call *spinning tops*. We nailed a piece of wood to the lid from a can of chemicals and ran behind it. Our toys were tires from the tractors and the tops from the chemical containers.

"But as it is written:
'What eye has not seen, and ear has not heard,
and what has not entered the human heart,
what God has prepared for those who love him,'"
—1 Corinthians 2:9, NABRE

GOD'S GRACE:

God will be our strength if we turn to Him. In life, a person may have to walk through difficult times. With a strong relationship with the Lord, a person can learn endurance. As our faith grows, we learn that God has a good future planned for us and we can begin to pray into that and agree with God about our future. God will begin to show us ways to bring change into our situation, He will open doors of opportunity, and we will begin to see real change in our lives if we continue to believe. Enduring the hard times without losing faith is not easy; but God is with us. Jesus walks with us if we invite Him to be with us. We do not have to be alone; nor do we have to come up with all of the solutions to our problems on our own. We can turn to the Lord and cry out for help. One important key is to not limit God on how to help us. It is important that we ask for help and then let God help us from His vast storehouse of riches.

"My God will fully supply whatever you need, in accord with his
glorious riches in Christ Jesus."
—Philippians 4:19, NABRE

CHAPTER TWELVE
HELP AND ENCOURAGEMENT

LARRY'S STORY:

In the morning, when we would hit the fields, the women would be singing. I did not get it at all. I was unsure why they were singing. Before I had any spiritual basis for understanding, I knew in my being that this singing was something special, but not understood by me at all at that time. There was definitely something deep and triumphant in their singing. The one song that I remember is, "I'll Fly Away." They sang soulfully, sounding more like, "I Fly Away."

I have to admit, when I first heard the singing, I was confused as to *why*. My mind saw those cotton balls like tiny clouds in a briar patch. Flying away was supposed to bring freedom, but among those endless rows, it was a far-reaching dream. Mostly the older women sang. Often other people would join them. While they were singing, everybody else working would be quiet. It was as if the others were respectful of the singing, or maybe pondering the words and the idea of flying away from bondage.

They would sing in the morning, but during the sweat of the day, during the break, there would be no singing; everybody was very business-like. When their voices switched off in the hot air, the loud noise of hidden insects rang free. As the dusk crept in and the work was almost over, the singers would start in again. There was no singing while we were riding on the truck. They would only sing as they were gathering or walking to the staging area to wait for the truck to come and bring us all back to our houses.

I did not know *why* this was; I just knew that was the *way* it was. In the beginning, I felt a hardness toward some of the singing. *What is there to sing about? This is a bad deal.* It was somewhat annoying because I did not understand the words. I could never figure out why they were singing through all that hard work. I did not understand the complexity of flying away at such a young age. I now understand that they believed that the Lord was literally going to come and snatch them up and away from their work, from the sweat, and from the heat. They believed they were going to be up in the air, in the beautiful blue sky.

If you were in a long row, chopping cotton, they would come and help, singing. It was a beautiful thing when I think of it today. The singers held their heads high, because they were singing a song of victory. It was a song of death, and yet of God's love overcoming death and overcoming everything that they were going through. Still, I wasn't even sure who or what God was.

When you heard one of the old people, who went through Jim Crow era and segregation, singing that song, they were testifying of a deep response to God delivering them out of some evil, torturous situation. I didn't know until much later that they had been through so much, yet they held on to their secret dignity that nobody could take away.

Many years later, after I became a Christian, I understood. It was then that I wanted to hear Mom sing, "I'll Fly Away." *She could sing!* I remember asking her sing it to me for three or four hours. I kept saying, "Mom, would you sing it again? Would you sing it again?" I seemed to enter into that song; I entered into the spirit of those words.

Whenever I hear that song today, it is a source of encouragement. I did not understand for a long time, but in a way, I was kind of like John Newton—I was blind, but now I see.

"Sing out, heavens, and rejoice, earth,
break forth into song, you mountains,
For the LORD comforts his people
and shows mercy to his afflicted."
—Isaiah 49:13, NABRE

GOD'S GRACE:

Sometimes the work and toil that we do on this earth can seem never ending, especially when we are doing hard labor with little choice or reward. As Christians, we know that we are called to work on this earth, yet we never have to forget that our reward is coming from God, not man. So, if we must deal with no thanks, little pay, or discouraging circumstances, we can remember that this life is temporary and that our true reward will be given to us by God, our Father.

Songs like "I'll Fly Away" help to remind us of this Truth during the darkest of times. Whatever we must survive on this earth, our eternal reward is still waiting; there will be a time of rest and refreshment, a time to sit at our Father's Table and feast, and an eternity to live with God. Singing to the Lord offers us an opportunity to not only worship God, but to remind us of His unfailing grace and mercy!

"Come to me, all you who labor and are burdened, and I will give you rest."
—Matthew 11:28, NABRE

CHAPTER THIRTEEN
MOURNING ON THE "MORNING BENCH"

LARRY'S STORY:

I went to church only a few times as a youngster. The little Baptist Church near us had something called the *morning* bench inside the church, or so I thought. It was in fact, the *mourning* bench. There was a bench where you were supposed to go and seek God.

Young kids were expected to sit on this bench and seek God. One evening, I went to the *mourning bench* service and found everybody crying with heavy emotion. The adults were all saying, "Look for a sign!" I thought it was all strange. Frankly, I thought the whole thing about God was just hocus-pocus.

People reported seeing signs in the sky, like six stars aligned in layers, or they saw the moon dance or something. I did not see anything. I was not buying it; I was not getting it. Nonetheless, I went on the mourning bench. I tried to seek God as best I knew but I felt nothing. I put some spit on my eyes to make it appear like I had been crying so people would see that I had indeed sought God.

> "The LORD is near to all who call upon him,
> to all who call upon him in truth."
> —Psalm 145:18, NABRE

GOD'S GRACE:

Jesus often invited the children to come to Him and even got mad at those who tried to stop the children from coming to speak to Him. While children may not be able to sit still for hours listening to a teaching, they can and will sit for a reasonable time learning about God's love and Jesus. Having a child-like faith is important for a Christian. It means that we listen with eagerness, that we ask questions and wonder about things, and that we go to Jesus about everything. What better way to learn about having child-like faith than by watching our children.

… but Jesus said, "Let the children come to me, and do not prevent them; for the kingdom of heaven belongs to such as these."
—Matthew 19:14, NABRE

LARRY D. ONEY

CHAPTER FOURTEEN
DETERMINATION

LARRY'S STORY:

My parents did not rant about being poor. It was just kind of, *this was the life*, and you did what you could. However, my mom apparently had gotten a taste of a different life. I did not know if it was because she went to visit her sister in the New Orleans area, but she saw another way of living. One day, something was stirring. Momma was talking about moving. She had set her mind on delivering her children from life on the plantation.

Moving brought up fears and a sense of instability in me because all I had ever known was living in our little house. It was a nervous time when she was talking about bringing us out of Holly Brook.

I remember my mother saying, "I'm gonna getchya' all outta here. I don't want ya'll to grow up like this." The boldness in her voice sent a clear signal that life was about to change. She was a very frank and direct person. She was not a fearful individual. She was not afraid of white people, men, or anything. Momma had been through a lot and had seen many things in life, which only made her stronger and more confident.

Determined to make a better life for us, my mom decided we were moving to Kenner, Louisiana. The journey began when she started moving us out in groups, taking the oldest boys first. Clifton, A.C., and George had to find work because they needed to secure housing for all of us. I had to stay back in the country with my sister, who was put in charge. My younger brothers and my younger sister stayed behind as well. Mom did not come and get us for almost a year. That was a horrible time. I continued working the field. My dad was rarely there. My sister cooked all the meals and tended to us all by herself. She did the best she could; she was now the "Momma."

It was a hard time with the family all separated. My dad was away. It was a troubling experience for me. I did not know what was going to happen next. I was filled with fear and anger. I cried a lot, but I did not let anybody see me crying. I know my sister was afraid too, but she did the best that she could. She would try to make sure we had something to bring to the field to eat. Sometimes when we were able to save a little extra money, she would bake a caramel cake. My sister was a good cook. She did her best to make our life good while we lived alone on the plantation.

"The LORD said to Abram: Go forth from your land, your relatives, and from your father's house to a land that I will show you."
—Genesis 12:1, NABRE

GOD'S GRACE:

When life seems hopeless, God is there to give us hope. God is present to be our strength and to help us hold on and to have the courage to stretch ourselves for the good of others. When we are weak, Jesus is our strength—He will carry us when we think that we cannot go any further.

"Do not be afraid." Jesus taught this throughout the Gospels. Fear can be terrorizing. It can keep us from even trying. Praying often can help. We are human and there are things in this world that can cause us to doubt and lose faith if we are not careful. Daily prayer can help us to remain firm in our faith and to grow in our understanding that we can trust God. Sometimes we just have to continue to repeat the truths that we have learned from God in order to have the courage and strength to see something through to the end.

The LORD is my light and my salvation;

whom should I fear?

The LORD is my life's refuge;

of whom should I be afraid?

—Psalm 27:1, NABRE

CHAPTER FIFTEEN
MOVING

LARRY'S STORY:

Finally the day came when it was my turn to leave the country. I was about ten years old. Sadly, James and Bobby did not join the family in Kenner for another two or three years since there was no work for them yet. I left with my mom, Uncle James, my sisters, and two younger brothers.

I remember tension in the air at the edge of the Civil Rights Movement. I was aware that something was going on with Dr. Martin Luther King, Jr. and with his marching. Dr. King had gone beyond what most black people in the Deep South could ever escape; constant fear that whites were going to do them some harm. Dr. King's words, "I am not afraid," rang in my mind.

We left Holly Brook with Uncle James, who was very kind to come and bring us to the New Orleans area. He had a truck, packed the whole bunch of us in, and ordered us to stay low. "You have to keep yo' heads down goin' through Mississippi cuz white folk will drag you out of the truck, and it's gonna' be trouble. We can't have a bunch of nappy–headed children sticking their heads up when we go through Mississippi."

I wondered why we had to keep our heads down. I tried to imagine what would happen if we did get stopped. *Is somebody going to be killed? Am I going to be killed? Are they going to kill my uncle? Are they going to kill my mom?* I remember being scared to death on that trip even though we were not stopped once during the long ride.

During that time there were a lot of unspoken rules that applied to black people. For example, it was understood that no more than one or two black males could be in a truck at one time. Blacks understood that to look white people in the eye was not allowed. It would be perceived as a threat that would bring immediate physical violence, or at the very least, a stiff reprimand. Many whites would have considered this as defiance—it was as if they thought we were staring them down.

My mom brought us out of the bondage of plantation life. She was like our Moses. She was our deliverer. The long trip from Lake Providence to Kenner was hectic, but we made it safely. Since there were so many of us in the truck, every moment we feared that the police would stop us and turn us over to the mean white men wearing sheets, the KKK.

After the agonizing excursion, I thought that I had escaped the oppressiveness of race and prejudice. Instead, I came to learn of a new, sophisticated apartheid system.

> "God is our refuge and our strength,
> an ever-present help in distress."
> —Psalm 46:2, NABRE

GOD'S GRACE:

A strong tree grows from a small seed, but it needs the right conditions to grow, such as: a safe place (so that wild animals don't dig it up), fresh water, sunlight, and the proper food and nutrients. We need the proper conditions as well in order to grow spiritually strong.

We need a safe place to learn about our faith—a place where we can ask questions without fear of being intimidated, and where the answers given are correct. We also need living water—Jesus said that He is the living water that we can drink from and our thirst will be quenched. Sunlight in one's spiritual life could represent the Holy Spirit—we all need the Holy Spirit to guide and teach us, and to move and work in us and through us to help us to become strong spiritually. A strong spiritual life also needs good spiritual food. The Word of God (the Bible) and the Bread from Heaven are what feeds and sustains us on this spiritual journey.

CHAPTER SIXTEEN
NEW PLACES

LARRY'S STORY:

I had the idea that in Kenner everybody lived in mansions like glass houses stacked on top of one another. I thought it would be just like *The Jetsons* cartoon. I imagined people floating around in cars in the air—that everything was just beautiful and perfect. What I found instead was a new kind of separation and discrimination. All of the black people lived segregated just like we did back on the plantation, except now the housing was much more expensive, a good deal smaller, and you had to pay rent to live in them.

Our large family all jammed into a three and a half room house on Milan Street which has since been torn down. All we had was a kitchen, bathroom, and one bedroom, but I was not complaining. I could not believe there was a toilet that actually flushed – *inside the house*! This was a big deal. There were no more midnight races to the outhouse in total darkness. There was no more running as fast as you could through rain or cold. Now we just had to wait for the person in line ahead of us or endure the pounding on the door when someone demanded that we "Hurry up!"

Even though things had not really changed for blacks, we had taken a tremendous leap from where we had come. I had never been in a house with a toilet inside of it. I later called this the Promise Land. There was indoor plumbing. *Praise God*!

There was a sink in the kitchen to wash the dishes, not a washtub. A bus took us to school, and not only did they give us something to eat for lunch, but we actually had a snack in the morning. There was food like I had never seen before! Still very little at home, but more food than we were ever used to.

Despite the tension and anxiety, my mom wanted us to get a good education and have access to decent work. Holly Brook, like Egypt, was a place where black people did not have the right to express themselves at all. In the Promise Land, as I like to call Kenner, black folk spoke and moved about in cars, lots of cars. In Egypt, you only made enough money for basic survival – for sustenance. In the Promise Land, even though the housing was not much better, there were possibilities and hope.

I could now work at my own pace mowing one or two yards. I was able to be as efficient as I wanted to be and I got to keep all the profit. I could not believe that we were actually being paid that much money to mow lawns. Even though this Promise Land (Kenner) was not really flowing with milk and honey, it was a world away from Egypt (Holly Brook Plantation). It was a fearful time for a young black person. There still was no one to nurture me or show me the ropes. The city was a new experience with so many people and cars and houses, and threats like drugs and guns. The general fear was in the unknown of this new place. However, I still would say that I would rather be in this Promise Land that was not so promising, than to be back in Egypt.

Although Kenner offered better opportunities for me than Holly Brook Plantation, it was still scary. There was no longer the security of being around people that I had known since birth. There were swarms of people everywhere. City life was altogether different from the country way of life that I was familiar with at Holly Brook. It seemed like many of the people in Kenner either had guns, drugs, or both. It was a different world all together. In a way, it *was* like *The Jetsons* cartoon; everything was new and wildly different.

My mom worked long hours, so again, she had no time to look after us children. The streets could very easily swallow you up. Mom was doing the best she could but she had to make a living for us.

"The LORD is good to those who wait for him,
a refuge on the day of distress,
Taking care of those who look to him for protection,"
—Nahum 1:7, NABRE

GOD'S GRACE:

As we try to help others, we begin to be part of the solution that raises people up from poverty; whether that poverty is financial or attention-time. We all need support and encouragement. As children of God, we need to look for those opportunities of need with others. Who may need a few minutes of our time? How can we encourage someone else?

He will shelter you with his pinions,

and under his wings you may take refuge;

his faithfulness is a protecting shield.

You shall not fear the terror of the night

nor the arrow that flies by day,

—Psalm 91:4-5

CHAPTER SEVENTEEN
BACK AND FORTH

LARRY'S STORY:

I was learning and experiencing in the Promise Land that if a person was willing to work hard, they would be paid decently for the work that they did. Going from making three dollars a day from sun up to sun down in the cotton fields, to making five dollars before noon, was a drastic change.

My job cutting grass with my cousin Nate went well for a while. I did most of the work. He told me what to do since I was just the country boy. We got cash on the barrelhead. I made five dollars in just three or four hours. I was rich for the first time in my life! I went right out and bought myself a milkshake and a hamburger, fully dressed with pickles and mustard, at the K & B drug store. I purchased them with my own money. It was wonderful. It was beautiful. However, it did not last.

After two years in Kenner, when I was about twelve years old, I was forced to go back to the plantation during the summer to work. My job cutting grass had slowed to nonexistent. I was taken back to Holly Brook where I worked the fields, allowing me to make a little money. I stayed with my Aunt Rosie B, or as we called her, *Roa-B*. It was good to be with relatives but I wanted to be with my own family in Kenner. I did not see James and Bobby because they were at our old house where my dad lived.

I never dreamed I would ever end up back in the cotton fields and re-enslaved in the bondage of Holly Brook plantation. But, there I was, back on Holly Brook, back in Egypt.

After a taste of life in the Promise Land, I hated the plantation more than ever. That first sight of those long rows of soybeans made me homesick for the life I left in Kenner. I missed my family and I missed my freedom. I remember being really sad at that time.

The worst job was chopping the weeds around the soybeans because there were always little brown snakes between the rows. My cousins, Freddie and Eddie, would simply chop the snakes in two and keep working the rows. I will never forget my mother coming to rescue me from the fields after a day filled with dodging the countless, little brown snakes. I am not a friend of snakes to this day.

Mom visited me on one occasion and saw the misery I was going through. She sent A.C. the following week to get me from the plantation and bring me back to Kenner. He had no reverse on his car. I remained glued to my seat during the entire four or five hour ride. Anything was better than dodging those snakes. A.C. did not bring James and Bobby back on the trip. There was no work for them yet. They stayed another two years in the country.

During our stay in Kenner, my dad came to stay with us for about a month. It was one of the happiest months of my life. Life seemed to have some kind of order again. But Dad did not stay long. One day he was just gone. We theorized among ourselves as to why he left so quickly. We came up with all sorts of ideas. The job in the glass plant where Dad worked was too hot. He longed for the open spaces in the country. He could not read. The traffic made him nervous. We thought up any reason why he would leave us. But we refused to let another possibility enter our minds. We refused to entertain the possibility that dad had rejected us for his other family that he had back in the country.

"Those who go forth weeping,
carrying sacks of seed,
Will return with cries of joy,
carrying their bundled sheaves."
—Psalm 126:5, NABRE

GOD'S GRACE:

The Church teaches: "Faith is certain. It is more certain than all human knowledge because it is founded on the very word of God who cannot lie." (*CCC* 157)

Having faith means that we are trusting in God, that we believe and trust God to work in our life with our best intentions in mind. Our faith in God can be nourished and grow as we begin to learn His Word and His ways. The more we learn about God, the more we learn that He is worth our trust. At times, God may invite us to do a certain action that might not make sense in the natural course of things; however, if we trust in Him, then we will learn that His ways are the best way. The Church also teaches that:

> Faith is an entirely free gift that God makes to man...To live, grow, and persevere in the faith until the end we must nourish it with the word of God' we must beg the Lord to increase our faith; it must be "working through charity," abounding in hope, and rooted in the faith of the Church. *(CCC* 162)

CHAPTER EIGHTEEN
WHO WILL YOU BE?

LARRY'S STORY:

During my early teenage years I was tall for my age; I took after my father in that respect. We all grow up wondering, especially during our teenage years, who and what we will be when we grow up. In retrospect, I see now that I was no different. The people that had the greatest respect in my neighborhood when I grew up were teachers. So I grew up, as a young teenager thinking (not out loud), only to myself, that I would be a teacher, like Ms. Clay or Mr. Nero, whom everyone held in high regard. I did not have the confidence to share that dream with anyone or let it come forth in my consciousness for too long.

In those years, I experienced racial prejudice on many occasions. The discussions in my neighborhood were primarily about racial prejudices, unfairness, and a lack of respect from whites toward blacks. There were marches, speeches on television, and for the first time, I understood what some of these messages were about. I was developing a consciousness about race and about the racial structures with its inequalities, indignities, and limitations if you were black.

One example of the indignities that blacks had to suffer was that my mother, who cleaned and cooked for a white family, was dropped off far from her neighborhood to walk a half of a mile home after working a full day, because her neighborhood was deemed "unsafe." Another example of the racial structural prejudice was the existence of a store that required black customers to purchase their items out of a window around the back rather than being allowed to come into the store.

I began noticing other things that I had not noticed before. Our neighbors often teased us. It did not matter that we were the same color as they were; they found a way to pick out our differences and make fun of us. We knew we sounded like a bunch of country bumpkins. They often said, "Ya'll sound country," and "Ya'll talk funny."

I remember thinking to myself, *Well you guys sound funny too*! I did not like some of these new people that we were living around. On the plantation, everyone at least tried to get along and look out for one another. In Kenner, it was a different story. I determined that I would try to learn to speak more clearly. When I eventually learned to speak decent English, a peculiar thing happened. Some of the people in my neighborhood were negative about it. They said, "Well, you talk proper like white folks."

I was not sure if I should be glad or angry. Whatever I did, it seemed I was not good enough; I did not measure up to someone's standards. Little by little, things began boiling inside me, not just because of this, but because of a combination of things. A subtle rage was stewing in my gut. I had no idea how hot the flame would get or how much longer it would be before the pot would boil over.

When I was a freshman in high school, I finally resolved that I really did not care what the black folk or the white folk thought of me, definitely not what the white folk thought. My toleration for any real or perceived prejudice from whites would make for fertile ground to grow the anger building inside of me.

"For those who are led by the Spirit of God are children of God. For you did not receive a spirit of slavery to fall back into fear, but you received a spirit of adoption, through which we cry, 'Abba, Father!' The Spirit itself bears witness with our spirit that we are children of God, and if children, then heirs, heirs of God and joint heirs with Christ, if only we suffer with him so that we may also be glorified with him."
—Romans 8:14-17, NABRE

GOD'S GRACE:

Unfortunately, there are people in this world who seem to constantly want to belittle others because they look different than they do. God is a God of beauty and variety, so He challenges us to embrace all of the shades of colors and hues that make up His creation.

"I praise you, because I am wonderfully made;

wonderful are your works!

My very self you know."

—Psalm 139:14, NABRE

Whether or not we talk different, or look different, God says in His Word, that we are created for a purpose. "For we are his handiwork, created in Christ Jesus for the good works that God has prepared in advance, that we should live in them." (Ephesians 2:10, NABRE)

CHAPTER NINETEEN
INJUSTICE

LARRY'S STORY:

I was beginning to get a feel for my neighborhood. When I was in the ninth grade my brother James finally came to live with us in Kenner. He and I were close and I felt relieved and glad to have him back with us and away from the plantation. We were all together now, except for my dad.

Life still seemed to hold many injustices. I had thought that everything was going to be so different. I left Holly Brook with the assumption that my family was going to live in a decent house and that everything would be wonderful. I was very wrong and continually disappointed. This Promise Land was hard. Widespread unemployment made life rough, not only for our family, but for most black families. The relentless undercurrent of crime forced us to be on guard in our surroundings. I still had the same fear of insecurity and instability that I felt on the plantation.

During this time, there was a lot of talk about Black Power. James Brown, a black music artist, had a popular record and some of the words were, "Say It Loud, I'm Black and I'm Proud." Many black people were uplifted by his song. It was a time of black consciousness and pride. This brought more change. A new sense of identity for the black people in the neighborhood started growing. A new identity started forming in me as well. A stronger sense of rebelliousness and defiance was boiling in me.

I decided that I wasn't going to be afraid of the police who would stop you for no reason, except that you were black in a white neighborhood; even if you were only there to cut the grass. As crazy as it may sound now, I was ready to die to fight indignity as I perceived it and was starting to not only talk about killing "blue-eyed devils" (white people), but was developing a desire to recruit others who shared my developing radical ideology.

In our poor neighborhood, there was a lot of strong talk on the corners about white people. It was mostly, "The white man did this," or "The white man did that." There was radical talk and radical thoughts. It became an ever-present idea that the blacks should take up arms, fight for justice, and fight for rights. I was listening to a lot of that. It was everywhere and I could not get away from it—and at the time, I didn't want to get away from it. It was shaping me into a more militant young man.

I understood now the dynamics of what was happening. I found myself shifting dangerously fast toward the radical side. With no real guidance, I listened to as much of the talk as I could. I developed a deep animosity toward whites and the dominance I felt they tried to hold over blacks. It was as if the Holly Brook landowner had followed us to Kenner and somehow multiplied himself. Now we were dominated by many instead of one.

"The LORD is my light and my salvation;

whom should I fear?

The LORD is my life's refuge;

of whom should I be afraid?"

—Psalm 27:1, NABRE

GOD'S GRACE:

Sometimes our enemies appear to multiply. Everything around us seems to aggravate us and we are not sure that anything is going our way. When we begin to walk with the Lord, even when we are faced with enemies, the Lord reminds us, as He did David, that even though we walk in the valley of the shadow of death, He is with us. By His power and grace, He will set a table before us in the presence of our foes. God can anoint our head with oil and cause our cup to overflow.

CHAPTER TWENTY
HIGH SCHOOL

LARRY'S STORY:

My high school days were at the very starting point of integration of the public schools. John Martin High School, the black high school in Jefferson Parish was closed down and black kids were suddenly forced to go to East Jefferson High School in Metairie, which was located in the wealthiest parish in the state at the time. Needless to say, we were not welcomed at the new school. It was like a war zone and blacks were the enemy, and whites were our enemies.

East Jefferson had over three thousand students. Less than two hundred and fifty students were black. That was my first major encounter with a large number of white people. The blatant discrimination that I came up against and saw was endless it seemed. Like the long, never ending rows of cotton with tall thick "Johnson grass." I began to hate whites in general, particularly early in high school. Our principal seemed like a racist, as were some of the teachers I encountered. There was definitely no Ms. Clay at East Jefferson.

I was a good student. I did my homework. I was a fast reader. High school was not any major challenge for me as far as learning went. I guess I did have some gift for retaining information because I did not have great study habits. There was no desk or quiet place in our house where I could sit down and study.

I was one of the few blacks in the ninth grade class. I remember one particularly humiliating experience with one of my teachers. He demanded that I explain to the whole class why black people did certain things. He wanted me to clarify why more black people did not work. He was asking questions that I could not even begin to answer. I was humiliated and embarrassed. He was degrading me in front of my entire class. This made me very angry at him. I hated that man for what he put me through. He was helping to fan the flames of rage and black militancy in me. For a very long time, I did not forgive him—it was not until I came to Christ that I was finally able to let go and forgive him. That was almost ten years later.

I found myself turning toward black militarism. I had a jacket with a Black Power fist on it. I wore that jacket with pride and confidence. I was now ready for any white person or authority figure to challenge me. I was growing strong in my convictions. I do not recall any of my siblings sharing my attitude about black power to the extreme measure that I did, certainly not my younger brothers. My older brothers were mostly involved with work.

The local sheriff said more than once that he would stop any and all blacks walking through white neighborhoods who had no business being there. There was national outrage but nothing really happened.

My brother James was a senior when I was a freshman. He got a job on Metairie Road. He was paid very little but he would always come and find me, and give me a portion of whatever he had earned so I could have something to eat. If James hadn't helped me out, I would have had to go to basketball practice on an empty stomach on many days. I was a starter on the team. I loved the game and played hard. Basketball was a good outlet for me to let out some of my frustration.

James had always been a very intense athlete himself. He liked basketball and could guard the bigger guys like a bulldog. He was very tough and very determined. He encouraged me in sports. I do not know how I would have made it without his devotion to my wellbeing. My dad was not in my life. In a way, James took his place. At least that was how I felt at the time.

"Do not fear: I am with you;

do not be anxious: I am your God.

I will strengthen you, I will help you,

I will uphold you with my victorious right hand."

—Isaiah 41:10, NABRE

GOD'S GRACE:

Each day as we build our relationship with God through prayer, it is a good practice to also pray for our enemies as Matthew 5:44 and Luke 6:27-28 teaches.

"But I say to you, love your enemies, and pray for those who persecute you"
— Matthew 5:44, NABRE

"But to you who hear I say, love your enemies, do good to those who hate you, bless those who curse you, pray for those who mistreat you."
— Luke 6:27-28, NABRE

LARRY D. ONEY

CHAPTER TWENTY-ONE
STANDING UP

LARRY'S STORY:

In my freshman and sophomore years of high school, I became the leader of a protest group. I can see that I wasn't exactly clear on what I was protesting, but it certainly grew out of the general atmosphere of racial injustice and racial prejudice that I felt. Our group was about fifty strong, all black students. It was not long before I boycotted the basketball team that I played on. I became the leader of the group. I was ready to be a warrior for Black Militarism. I was becoming a Black Radical! I was determined that I was not going to stand by and let whites or the white establishment (the principal, the coaches, and the teachers) dictate my life any longer.

I told my coach that I thought it was unfair that we did not have any black cheerleaders for the team since the team was mostly black students. My coach, who was a good man, understood my position but was powerless to do anything about it. After a month or so, little by little, most of the players went back, and ultimately, I went back as well. The school principal held the idea that *majority rules* on all counts. He did not respect the welfare or dignity of any race except the whites. He and I constantly were at odds with one another.

The principal and I would discuss things but nothing would change. Whenever we would have football games at home, I would wear my Black Power jacket with the sleeves cut out with a clench fist, so that he would understand that I saw him as the enemy and that he and I were at war.

I felt that I had to lead the marches and protests of unfair treatment toward black students. We did not have any representation with cheerleaders or the student body of the sister school. No one stepped up to help us. No one spoke up about the obvious unfairness involved. I was compelled to take a stand. I called for a protest march over the racism that I felt existed at East Jefferson. I was not going to keep quiet or look the other way. When I announced my plans to the television stations and they showed up, we had posters and banners. I told the principal that there was going to be an armed conflict. He threatened to have me arrested, but I was not arrested.

I was not afraid to go to jail. I knew someone had to stand up against the racial injustices we were enduring. I picked my words just like I had picked cotton; no one led me by the hand, no one showed me what to do. The principal and I understood one another. It was a power struggle and he held all of the power. I had no fear of him. He was very cautious of me and made sure the assistant principals kept an eye on me.

"For you were called for freedom, brothers. But do not use this freedom as an opportunity for the flesh; rather, serve one another through love."
—Galatians 5:13, NABRE

GOD'S GRACE:

Everyone wants to be listened to and heard. What you have to say is important. It is also critical that we learn to listen to others because what they have to say can be important as well. As we listen to others, our viewpoints might change, but even if they don't, we still may come to understand why that person feels the way that he does.

Listening to others is also a great way to show that they are valuable. It is important to pay attention to those around us. Jesus taught us the importance of love. By listening closely to others, we can discover what each person around us needs in order to feel respected and loved. Everyone is different and unique and we need to celebrate those differences and learn to appreciate what others have to offer.

CHAPTER TWENTY-TWO
SUPPORT

LARRY'S STORY:

I do not know how my mom felt about me leaning strongly toward becoming a black militant. She didn't go marching around the house saying, "Say it Loud, I'm Black and Proud" or anything like that, but she clearly understood indignity and unfairness, because she had probably had experienced it many times herself.

Mom had to go and meet with the principal once. I was being suspended for refusing to go back to class, choosing to protest instead. The principal demanded that she come to school and try to get me to curtail my protesting activities, speech giving, and exhorting others (mainly the black students) not to go to class.

Her coming to the school was a hardship. My mom did not drive. She had never driven once in her whole life. We had to get somebody to bring her to school. My older brother, Cliff took off work and drove us to school in his old beat-up car and then brought both of us back home. The principal wanted to give me a three-day suspension, but mom persuaded him otherwise. So I had no suspension, but it did establish a fragile truce between the principal and myself. It would not last.

Mom did not try to stop me from being involved in protesting. I don't know if she had the capacity to do so. We had been in the city now for four years or so. Mom had to work cleaning houses. She had to walk to catch the bus, and then hopefully get a ride back, at least close to the house, if not all the way to the house, by the people that she worked for. I do not know where my father stood on my attitude. He was back on Way Way Plantation. He was not in my life. At school, Mom was respectful and dignified before the principal but she was clearly not afraid and I was not afraid either.

"Before they call, I will answer;

while they are yet speaking, I will hear."

—Isaiah 65:24, NABRE

GOD'S GRACE:

Everyone needs support. Church, prayer groups, and Bible study groups can all be a good source of support and encouragement for our daily walk. It is important for Christians to have safe places of support during difficult times. When we are enjoying the peaceful times in our lives, we can offer support and encouragement to others. Finding places where we can feel comfortable and safe to explore our spiritual life can be very beneficial. Finding those places where we can contribute and receive support are valuable.

LARRY D. ONEY

CHAPTER TWENTY-THREE
HARASSMENT

LARRY'S STORY:

With all my mom had to do, it was just too tough to keep up with such a large family. During that time, we had moved from our first little house. We were now living on Atlanta Street, which butted up against the levee of the Mississippi River, near a place called Charlie's Blue Room (a bar). It was a dangerous place. For the first time in my life, I saw a guy with a needle hanging out of his arm. I knew that guy's brother. I never went into Charlie's Blue Room. I was afraid to even walk by there, but I had to stand beside it every morning to get the bus.

I tried to join the Black Panther party in New Orleans because I felt the whites in our area were so doggedly oppressive. I figured we should kill the ones that were unfair to blacks. I wanted to be the one who decided which ones should be killed. Thanks to God's amazing grace, I couldn't come up with enough money to get a bus ticket and go find this group operating in New Orleans.

I was regularly stopped by the Jefferson Parish police for no other reason except that I was walking through a white neighborhood after basketball practice. We had to catch the bus by walking through a white neighborhood where the school was and then walking the rest of the way home after the bus dropped us off at the edge of our neighborhood. We had no choice; it was the way home. Police officers would always stop us and search us. They would question us, wanting to know what we were doing there. The policemen assumed that I was the leader of the group and I guess I was. From ninth grade through twelfth grade, that seemed to be my identity. We were ordered to put our hands on the car and spread our legs like criminals. It was ongoing general harassment. Avoiding the police was like trying to dodge those little brown snakes back in Holly Brook. We were accustomed to being stopped, questioned, and often searched, not only on our way from school, but also in our own neighborhoods. When we had to catch the bus home from basketball practice, from the white neighborhood to the black neighborhood, we could never stand at the bus stop because we were targets.

Some of the young white guys would throw bottles and other things out the windows of their cars if someone stood there, so we would wait for the bus to get closer, and then run up to it, hoping that the bus would wait so we could catch a ride to our neighborhood. Our lifestyle had become a life of skirting around whites and being treated like criminals. The hatred inside me grew.

It was hard to suppress those feelings. It was more than a challenge to ignore the radical ideas that had been festering for such a long time. Then my mindset took an unexpected turn and slowly began to change.

"The LORD is a stronghold for the oppressed,

a stronghold in times of trouble."

—Psalm 9:10, NABRE

GOD'S GRACE:

Living in a community where oppression seems to come from all sides, a place that leaves a person in constant fear and anxiety, can take a toll. Where can we turn to find peace and rest? God offers us peace beyond our situation.

> "For God will hide me in his shelter
>
> in time of trouble,
>
> He will conceal me in the cover of his tent;
>
> and set me high upon a rock."
>
> —Psalm 27:5, NABRE

CHAPTER TWENTY-FOUR
THANKSGIVING

LARRY'S STORY:

On Thanksgiving Day my whole family was together except for A.C. who stayed back in the country for work. The November holiday sparked a new idea in my thinking. We had nothing to eat but we were happy. We had indoor plumbing, a toilet that actually flushed most of the time, and one of those party-line black rotary dial phones. Our house was small, cramped, and in need of repair but we were together. We never lived in a housing project; we always lived in a house. My brother James and I would talk about how we felt like that was a gift to never have had to live in a project. We were right next to a project but not in one (no offense is intended toward the many good people that had to and still do live in a project housing development).

We did not have any food on this Thanksgiving Day except for some greens. Then there was a knock at the door. No one moved for several seconds. It felt like time stopped. Somebody opened the door revealing a white woman holding a bag of groceries. She had red hair and manicured fingernails. My mother was never a racist; but she always said we had to be careful around white people. We all just stood there looking at each other. I wondered about the white woman's motives. I wondered if she was going to turn us over to the landlord. There was always a concern that the landlord would demand more rent if he knew that ten people were living in a house that was meant for four or five. *Why did she come on Thanksgiving Day?*

One of my brothers went to the door and received the bags. We could not believe it! The bags were full of bread, all kinds of stuffing, fresh duck, and smoked oysters in a can. We had never tasted canned oysters, which we assumed had to be something very special. We could not afford oysters in the can or otherwise. Clearly, she had just been to the grocery store, purchased these groceries, and brought them to our house.

Nobody knew who this woman was. It had been our understanding that when white people knocked on the door, it was the police, a gas leak, a fireman, a bill collector, or just plain trouble. However, out of all the poor people in our neighborhood, somebody with a bag of groceries was on our doorstep. To us, she seemed like an angel of mercy bringing us provisions on Thanksgiving Day. She gave us the groceries with a warm smile and then suddenly, she was gone.

There I stood, a young, angry black man, growing into a hardcore radical. I had a Black Power fist on my shirt, a big afro, a mean look on my face, and was ready to take up arms against whites. I was bent on finding the Black Panther Party to take up arms and kill white people. Now, I was confounded. This knock on the door by some strange woman was the first sign that God's amazing grace was rushing in helping me to overcome the power of race in my life. I realize now, looking back, that this woman was on an assignment from God. As she came to my family, God's grace was coming into my life through her unforeseen act of kindness.

Inevitably during Thanksgiving, we speak of this unknown woman and we all agree that she was a messenger from God, an angel doing God's bidding. I see now that this woman with fiery red hair was one of the arrows in the quiver of the Lord and she allowed herself to be used by Him. I could not hate her. Her skin color marked her as an enemy, but for no reason, she had just brought us much needed food. She was like an angel bringing us sustenance and relief. My mom and sisters cooked up a great meal and we all ate until we were filled. It was a memorable day that will always stand out to me and my whole family.

"My God will fully supply whatever you need, in accord with his glorious riches in Christ Jesus."
—Philippians 4:19, NABRE

GOD'S GRACE:

Sometimes it only takes one act of kindness in the name of Jesus to set off a chain reaction of kindness in others. The woman who gave me and my family food for Thanksgiving was not only supplying food for a meal, but food for thought. I began to see that not all people with white skin were bad. Jesus had given me the opportunity to make a change in my thought process, and I took it.

Jesus can open our eyes to see more than what we can see on our own. I truly believe that God often sends angels disguised as people into our lives and sometimes we do not recognize them. In the same way, sometimes, we think that our little acts of kindness or our warm smile mean nothing, but often they have the power to soften a hard heart and to redirect a young mind.

CHAPTER TWENTY-FIVE
CHANGE

LARRY'S STORY:

Right up to the point of my graduation, I was still very radical. The irony in that was, when I was a junior, my predominantly white junior class voted me "Mr. Junior Class." I found myself slowly giving whites the benefit of the doubt mainly because of this white woman who had extended grace to our family. I could not say that all of my hatred of whites had totally dissipated yet, but after the scene at our house with the groceries and our surprise visitor it was starting to fade.

Life circumstances had conditioned me to believe that all white people were bad. In fact, we called white people, "blue-eyed devils" because we felt that they were like devils and could not be trusted.

I excelled at basketball and received several scholarship offers. I accepted the one to McNeese State University in Lake Charles, Louisiana. I knew I was fortunate. I had a way to get a college education. My two brothers, who are next in age after me (James and Bobby), caught the bus every day after school to go to work for various people cutting their grass and cleaning around their houses to help me as best they could while I was in college.

My older brother, James, began sending me five or ten dollars in the mail. I think he was proud of me when I got the basketball scholarship. James supported me in every way. Even though I had the scholarship, I still needed things like snacks, toothpaste, and miscellaneous items. He would send me whatever he could. He was always very good to me and generous with his money. During the first year of college, I found the level of my maturity calming. For the first time, I began to slip deeper into studies and farther from radical ideas. I made the Dean's List several times. My hardest transition time was as a freshman, but overall I did well in college.

"He will wipe every tear from their eyes"
— Revelation 21:4, NABRE

GOD'S GRACE:

Just as it helps us to be encouraged, it also helps others to be encouraged by us. When we offer encouragement to other people, we are beginning a culture of encouragement. Others will offer encouragement in return. We are designed to encourage and help one another—we are designed to live in communities. Be the first to offer someone encouragement. Offer someone sincere encouragement about his/her school work, sports, at the office, or at church whenever you come into contact with him for one or two weeks. Watch the results. The person will begin to stand up straighter, smile, and feel better about himself. Perhaps the person will begin to encourage others.

As the culture of encouragement begins to take hold, we will begin to notice that others begin to offer encouragement as well, and the negative unhelpful criticism begins to decline. As we live out our Christian faith in all areas of our life, we need to offer encouragement to those around us. Encouragement can take many forms: an email letting someone know how much he has meant to you, a phone call sharing your appreciation for the hard work completed, encouraging someone to continue with a Bible study, or expressing interest in something that is important to another person. We should try to express ourselves in a positive way and consider encouraging someone today!

CHAPTER TWENTY-SIX
A CALL

LARRY'S STORY:

During summer break, I came home for a visit and helped my brothers with their grass cutting and cleaning jobs. We were still confronted with racial slurs as we waited for the bus to take us home from work. We were used to having glass soda bottles and beer bottles thrown at us from passing cars and trucks while we stood on Metairie Road. Every day that we made it home without being called the "n" word and not being injured was a good day.

One of the older white couples across the street from where I worked gave me some used plates and other utensils to bring home for doing a good job on her yard. They knew that I had to walk through their white neighborhood to catch the bus so they gave me a note explaining that they had given me these plates and other utensils. They knew that any young black man walking through a neighborhood near Metairie Road would certainly be stopped by the police and arrested on theft charges unless they had a note of explanation or something. It was a given fact that someone would have accused me of stealing those things if I did not have that note. I had a nervous feeling in my stomach all the way home. The reality of the social situation we found ourselves in was daunting.

To escape the demoralizing constraints for an afternoon, my brothers and I decided to go fishing near the Gulf of Mexico one day. We caught the ferryboat and crossed the Mississippi River. On the boat with my brothers, this man came up to me and said, "I saw you, and I see that God is doing something in your heart. God has been waiting for you to give your heart to Him."

I was stunned! I did not understand what he was saying or what was happening. I thought the whole thing was strange. I figure the guy was one of those religious fanatics even though he did not seem fanatical. He acted and spoke very calmly to me. While he spoke, I just stood there trying to seem casual. As the ferryboat was crossing the Mississippi River, I leaned on the rail, trying not to seem too bewildered.

I realize now that the guy was simply riding back and forth waiting for people. He was a fisherman of men! He was preaching the Word, and inviting people to come to the Lord. The ferryboat was his pulpit and I was one of the fish he was trying to catch. He did it calmly but convincingly, with conviction but not with great emotional fervor or anything—at least not on the outside. I was speechless. That was the first time I was publically evangelized. Somebody was actually witnessing to me about the Lord. In my heart, I felt that God was speaking through that man. I never met him again; I had no idea who he was. I can now see that this was a Sovereign move, or some kind of sovereign act of God. The man gave me a tip, a Holy Spirit tip that God wanted to do something in me.

I kept waiting for someone else to speak to me the way the man on the ferry boat had spoken to me. I was waiting for some follow-up person to tell me more. My heart was starting to open to the move of God. I wanted more. I wanted to hear another Word from God. It shook me to the core for many months. I contemplated, in my ignorance and lack of understanding, about what the man had been saying; that God had been looking for me and wanted me to give my heart to Him. I had no idea or understanding of what that meant. I did not tell my brothers. I did not tell anybody. I was not even sure what in the world was going on inside me. I felt an unmistakable void inside me for the first time and felt that it was somehow connected to the message that the man on the ferry had given me. Looking back now, I can see how this encounter on the ferry boat and many other encounters had brought me to a place where my heart was beginning to open to the action of God's Holy Spirit.

"In all circumstances give thanks, for this is the will of God for you in Christ Jesus."
—1 Thessalonians 5:18, NABRE

GOD'S GRACE:

Expressing thanks is another essential piece to a healthy spiritual life. God has given us so much—some things that we know about and some things that we have not yet learned of—and it is imperative that we take the time to give thanks. Conveying our thanks to God is not only for God's benefit, but for our own. As we thank God for the individual things that He has blessed us with and for His movement in our lives, we begin to see just how much He has done for us. This helps us to grow in our faith—we see what God has already done and we begin to trust more and more that He will continue to be a part of our lives.

Every morning as you prepare for your day, list three things that you are thankful that God has blessed you with in the last week. Start big and then work your way to the individual things. For example, one morning you might thank God for: that you are alive, for the sunshiny day, and for the gift of your family. As you become more familiar with this practice, you may find yourself thanking God for your ability to get so much done at work the day before, healing the soreness in your back, or helping you to have patience with your children that week. God wants to be a part of our lives.

CHAPTER TWENTY-SEVEN
MARRIAGE

LARRY'S STORY:

After my first two years of college in the southwestern part of the state, I switched schools. I decided to go to Nicholls State University. I was a typical college student, searching for my place in life. While I attended Nicholls, my brother James would take his old car, and drive up to get me during the breaks to come home, because it was only about two hours away from where he lived.

After all the other boys had left home, James put off being married and stayed to support my mother at the house. He delayed his own life and took care of Mom and the house out of his own means. The house was still a gathering place, but it was all done with James' work and finances.

I went to college for my first two years, at McNeese State in Lake Charles. I finished my second two years at Nicholls State in Thibodaux, Louisiana. There, I met, dated and married a woman who was from a different cultural and ethnic background than I was from. She was an artist and our classes happened to be in the same building.

My new wife and I moved to Boulder so that I could begin studying at the University of Colorado at Boulder. I was intent on getting a PhD in Psychology. I do not know why I chose psychology. The decision was probably based on somebody describing it to me as the "helping profession." I liked the idea of helping people and saw psychology as a way to do that. I had the idea that I wanted to teach Psychology at the college level, or be a Clinical Psychologist. I mainly wanted to teach.

Even after I got out of school and started to work, I still thought at some point, that I would go back and try to get my PhD. I loved the idea of education, teaching, and learning. I thoroughly enjoyed college and the engagement with the professors and the other students.

I was living free from the poverty that I had always known. I had a job and a good car. We were a young couple just getting started, but we had a good life.

"Before they call, I will answer;

while they are yet speaking, I will hear."

—Isaiah 65:24, NABRE

GOD'S GRACE:

Each person has natural gifts and talents that God gave to them at birth. There are spiritual gifts that God has given as well to each person. Learning what our gifts and talents are (natural and spiritual) are an important step in our spiritual journey. We need to learn what our gifts are, use and practice our gifts, and grow in our gifts, just like an athlete who practices his/her sport. As we grow in our gifts, we are able to find our place in the Body of Christ.

A house is not built of only one piece of wood. It takes many. We make up the House of God—the Body of Christ—the Church. We cannot stand alone, we need each other. Every gift is needed and we need a variety of people with those gifts to help build the Kingdom of God. As 1 Corinthians 12:4-26 explains, we are all different parts of the same body and we are all needed. If one person is a "foot" and they decide to be an "eye" then who will be the foot and what will the one that was supposed to be an "eye" do? We are all gifted with a different set of gifts and they are all valuable to the Body of Christ. Finding our gifts, using them wisely, and growing in them is a way for us to help build the Kingdom of God.

CHAPTER TWENTY-EIGHT
QUEST FOR GOD

LARRY'S STORY:

At one point, my wife and I were living in a suburb of New Orleans. After two or three years, I was progressing with the company that I was working for and they soon offered me a manager's job in Lake Charles, Louisiana. We moved there and rented a house. I had more money and a better job than anybody in my family at that time. I was the first person to get a college degree and have a professional level job in my family. My wife and I had money to buy extra, like seafood as well as our first new car. We did not really like living in the Lake Charles area and after a couple of years we decided to move.

We found a quaint old house in Ponchatoula that we decided to buy. We had good credit, we bought our first house, and we had two beautiful children. However, I had a nagging feeling of sadness inside. Even though I did have quite a bit of time with my family since we were closer to them now, we were mostly just living our lives without God in it like most of the people with whom we were acquainted. We seldom went to church, even though my wife had been a Catholic her whole life.

I was feeling like there had to be more to life. The emptiness I felt caused me to speculate about whether my father's absence had anything to do with my sadness. My dad never saw me play basketball in junior high school, high school, or in college. He did not know that I got the Scholastic Award on my team as a senior in college; he was not there. He never knew that I was on the Dean's List. He was not in my life during junior high school and through my college years. This sad fact and his continuing absence in my life certainly added to the sadness and emptiness that I was experiencing.

I do not know what fully sparked it, but I began my quest for God. I did not recognize it then, but I know now that it was the Holy Spirit; God was missing in my life. At twenty-five years old, I was having my own adult "mourning bench" experience. I read the Bible from front to back without gaining any understanding. I was simply searching. My wife tried to help.

Part of my search involved listening to radio programs. I would listen to anything that had a religious connotation. I was looking for anything to clear up the questions swirling around in my mind. I started listening to religious programs on the radio every day to and from work.

In the throes of my search, I felt a sorrow—I had a house, a car, a good job, and I was doing well on the job (I'm advancing); and yet I was still sad. I did not know where this emptiness was coming from. My wife and I were living about thirty-five minutes away from where my family was in Kenner. We were pretty much living on our own because it was a different lifestyle from how the rest of my family was living. They were closer to the city, and we were in a little town, a rural area away from the city. I often drove down to meet with my brothers to go fishing.

I realized that I was not as strong on the race issue. My mind had turned to deeper things. I wanted to know something; I wanted to know something about the Bible and about God. All I could do was read the Bible. As I read, I learned a lot of scripture but I did not gain much understanding.

I do not remember how long it took me to read the Bible but it did not seem like it took that long. I read it like you read a novel, so I did not retain much, but apparently, I retained more than I thought. I did not know exactly what I was searching for, except maybe for the meaning of my life.

I do not know if my college psychology classes had any role in me looking for something deeper; they may have. However, I really believe that it was just a sovereign move of God—a heart searching for God, and God searching for a heart that wants to receive Him. I know now that this is called "grace;" which is unmerited favor given from God through circumstances and people.

"Then the LORD will guide you always

and satisfy your thirst in parched places,

will give strength to your bones

And you shall be like a watered garden,

like a flowing spring whose waters never fail."

—Isaiah 58:11, NABRE

GOD'S GRACE:

Fellowship is another important aspect of a strong spiritual life. We can decide what we want our lifestyle to be and then hang around with people that support that lifestyle. Christian fellowship is another way that we can grow closer to the Lord. By sharing our time, talent, and gifts with others, we are helping to further the Kingdom of God. As Christians, when we look into someone else's face, we should see the face of Christ. We are called to be servants—we are called to serve those in need. There are times when we are able to serve others, and then there are times when we are in need of being helped. By living in fellowship with other Christians, we are able to help each other grow and to stay on the right path, so that when we do have to go out into the world, we are able to stand strong in our faith despite the temptations. Christianity is a communal faith. Christians belong to a community of faith— both our local church and the larger Christian community.

LARRY D. ONEY

CHAPTER TWENTY-NINE
NOT MY WAY

LARRY'S STORY:

My neighbor at that time happened to be a salesman. He was also a Mormon. One day he was at my house. It seems that my neighbor thought that I could be a good salesman. I told him that I could not do any selling for him. "I don't have time to sell at your company; I have to get my life right with God." It was like the words gushed out on their own. I could not believe they came from me.

My neighbor nodded, appearing to agree with me. He acted like he had the answers that I needed. He said, "Listen, I'm going to send these two guys to your house. They can help you find what you are looking for. They know all about God."

Before I knew it, two young Mormon men were in my house telling me all about God. I listened to them because my heart was open. They were talking to me and not to my wife because she did not want any part in Mormonism. I remember one of them saying,

"Oh, Mr. Oney, if you read Chapter 32 in the Book of Mormon you will find that Joseph Smith is really the right way to go and that Mormonism is the right way to go."

I had not been a person of faith at all. I hadn't gone to church with my wife very much. And all of a sudden, these young men were coming twice a week and spending an hour or two with me talking about faith and becoming a Mormon. It sounded good to me.

Today, I know that when a searching heart is open, we, as the Body of Christ, should be ready to share our faith. My heart was open when the two Mormons showed up and I wanted to receive God. Up to that point, nobody had presented Jesus Christ as the Son of the living God to me in any detail and these Mormons were saying Joseph Smith was the way to God. I was buying what they were selling.

I was not sure what to do. My neighbor explained that the Book of Mormon was "The Way." I read their book with an open mind but all the while, somehow I heard in my heart, *"It is not true."* Yet, I was still listening, still searching. I read chapter 32 of the Book of Mormon and asked God, "If you are real, if you really exist, let me know that this is the way that I should go." I know now that I was "praying" without even being really aware of what prayer was.

I was about to take the step toward becoming a Mormon when my wife got nervous. She did not know anything about Mormonism, but she did not feel that I should be going in that direction and that what I was searching for would not be found in Mormonism.

She called a Catholic deacon who was a friend of hers and later became a dear friend of mine. He had to hurry as I was going to be baptized into the Mormon Church in three days. The deacon came over and shared information on the Catholic faith with me. He began to teach me about the Catholic Church. He patiently shared his faith with me and answered my many questions. As a result, I rejected the Book of Mormon and continued my journey toward faith and ultimately becoming a Catholic Christian.

"I will instruct you and show you the way you should walk,

give you counsel with my eye upon you."

—Psalm 32:8, NABRE

GOD'S GRACE:

Scripture teaches us that we should desire "meat not milk." (See 1 Corinthians 3:2) Really spending time with one Scripture passage to digest what it means is vital. From time to time, everyone comes across a Scripture that causes them to pause and think, "*I may understand this Scripture; however, I know that this Scripture is important and I'm just not getting it all.*" (or something similar).

It is important that when we come across a Scripture like this that we deal with it by praying about it. Asking the Holy Spirit to enlighten us, or asking what it should mean, or how it should affect our lives in a real and personal way. This may take days, weeks, or even months. Don't give up. Don't stop praying for revelation, or "chewing" on it. When we begin to get something or begin to understand it—we need to stay with it until we discern that we have everything that God wants to give us **at this time**.

Also, years from now, we may come across the same Scripture and find that God wants to teach us something different about it. It does not mean that we "missed" something earlier. God is gentle and He only gives us what we can handle at the time. And occasionally we need to learn about something else and then come back to a Scripture to learn more.

Overall, remember: every Scripture is both "milk" and "solid food." Every Scripture offers us an encounter with the Word Made Flesh—Jesus Christ. As we "chew" over a Scripture and think about it, we are reflecting on the Lord and our relationship with Him.

CHAPTER THIRTY
A RETREAT

LARRY'S STORY:

I was still not quite fully on board with the Catholic thing; when my wife wanted me to go on a retreat, there were intense negotiations. I thought we were just going to a meeting. I had never been on a retreat in my life. I did not want to go. I went to this event, a place where I had never been before at a retreat center on the North Shore of New Orleans. I did not want to go on this retreat. In fact, I tried to say that my stomach was upset and I would probably only stay for one day. I had never gone anywhere where you actually sleep at another place, and it was about religion.

We had a lady named Hattie babysit our children while we were gone. Hattie was a strong young black woman who had several kids of her own. We felt safe leaving the kids with her. She was a good cook, a good housekeeper, and a great woman of God. She was a strong woman of faith. She loved our children. So I had no excuses. God had boxed me in.

On the retreat, I mainly tried to stay out of the way. I thought the whole thing was very weird. People were praying in a strange way, that I now know was their prayer tongues. People were going to Mass and Communion. Everybody seemed to be beaming, or very happy, kind of calm and peaceful. My wife seemed very happy too.

I found myself lost at this retreat. I tried to hang back and just be invisible. Out of nowhere, this short, smiling woman with blond hair named Sue came right up to me. I was just trying to avoid people. (Sue would later become my godmother.) She came up and looked me in the eyes with her piercing eyes. Sue could somehow see things. She knew things about me before I said a word. She presented herself like a faith-filled child. She was very bright—there was brightness about her person. It was not the whiteness of her skin that bothered me, but the uncanny way she could sense that my heart was troubled. Sue just came over and asked me, "How are you doing?"

I said, "Alright."

"It doesn't look like you are doing alright." And then she said, "God loves you, Larry."

I thought, *I don't even know her ... she just met me ... how does she know my name?* For no apparent reason, I immediately began to cry and I could not stop. I had no idea why. I did not know what was happening to me. She told me three simple words that I will never forget. She said, "God loves you." I believe that was the first time anybody had ever said those words to me.

"For the LORD gives wisdom,

from his mouth come knowledge and understanding;"

—Proverbs 2:6, NABRE

GOD'S GRACE:

Going away on a retreat means that one goes to a specific place (usually quiet and away from the distractions of this world) and stays for a length of time to "be with God" and to "consider spiritual matters." For some, the hardest part is being away from the distractions of the world (which usually means: no cell phones, computers, games, TV, or magazines). Once a person gets over the culture shock of that, usually they relax and just go with it. There are Retreat Houses or places that host retreats for groups and/or individuals, but it is not necessary for one to go to a Retreat House to have a successful retreat. Also, the length of a retreat is different for every person and their needs at the time. For some, a half-day retreat can be just as fulfilling as a week-long retreat for someone else. Usually, it is good for one to start with short one to two-hour retreats, and then, over time, work up to longer retreats as needed.

For those who are trying to make big decisions or discern something important, a longer retreat may be necessary. For example, if you are trying to discern if you should get married, which college you should go to, to have a child, or if you should go away on a missionary trip, a longer retreat may be necessary (a week or more).

For most of us, in our daily life, it is good to "get away" at least once every month or two and offer God our undivided attention for at least half of a day (4 hours or so). This allows us to step away from everyday life and take a look at the big picture. This time away offers us a time of refreshment, but also a time where we can hear from the Lord about our lives.

Some retreats are "guided" and they have a set theme that will walk one through some Scriptures (based on the theme of the retreat), perhaps guided meditation, and/or some individual time (for private prayer, the Sacrament of Reconciliation, etc...). Individual retreats can be very beneficial because one can set one's own pace (although it is always good to have a plan before you start to guide you). On an individual retreat, one can choose the Scriptures that pertain to what they are trying to discern. Also, quiet time to pray is a key component that allows us to experience God's love and grace in a special way.

CHAPTER THIRTY-ONE
SCRIPTURE

LARRY'S STORY:

On the retreat, I got a hold of a Bible and the first Scripture I read that had any meaning to me was John 6:54, which says: "Whoever eats my flesh and drink my blood has eternal life, and I will raise him up on the last day." (NABRE)

When I read that Scripture from John, I knew that the Eucharist was real. I knew this Church was where I needed to be. I knew at that moment that I was going to become a Catholic. I had been nothing, as far as faith was concerned. I had just been a wanderer. I was a lost soul. Now, I was found. The eyes of my understanding were being enlightened and I was beginning to know "the hope of His calling" like the prayer in Ephesians 1:18 that the deacon had explained in my catechism.

> "May the eyes of [your] hearts be enlightened, that you may know what is the hope that belongs to his call, what are the riches of glory in his inheritance among the holy ones." (Ephesians 1:18, NABRE)

I saw the bread lifted up and a priest proclaiming it as the "Lamb of God, who takes away the sins of the world," and, "Happy are we that are called to the Lamb's Supper."

I was finally seeing with eyes of faith, as if my eyes were suddenly opened. This was Jesus Christ that was being praised and lifted up. This was Communion! I was realizing the First Supper, the Lord's Supper. I was realizing that this Sacrifice was the same one that Jesus offered at Calvary.

I was caught up in John 6:53b-54, "unless you eat the flesh of the Son of Man and drink his blood, you do not have life within you. Whoever eats my flesh and drinks my blood has eternal life, and I will raise him on the last day." (NABRE) At that moment, I believed that I was supposed to become a Catholic. I did not know how I knew that. *I just knew.* There is a knowing, by The Spirit and I knew that God had called me home to the Catholic Church (even though I barely knew much about it). I knew this was what I wanted.

I desired the Eucharist (Communion) and I believed that it really was the Body and Blood, Soul and Divinity of Jesus Christ. My wife was very happy for me. A great thirst welled up in me for the Eucharist. I felt exuberant! I felt caught up in something mystical. My heart was overjoyed, feeling the love of God—His light, His glory, His peace, and His joy surrounded me. I desired the Eucharist. I still had a long way to go, but God, by His sovereign will, and by His grace, was sweeping me up into something.

I had once told my wife that I would never become a Catholic. I told her she could raise the children Catholic, but "Catholics are just too weird for me." I could not get over the fact that they *eat flesh* and *drink blood*. Cannibalism is evil, or illegal, or something! *It had to be*.

Now, I was seeing Catholics go to Communion and get a little piece of bread, and drink from a common cup. I had this strange knowing that this was not cannibalism. This truly was the Lamb of God; this was the Lord! In an instant, all doubt was erased. That was one of the life-changing events in my life.

Years later, I came to learn that the Holy Spirit was moving in my heart and in my life. He was the One leading me and revealing truth to me, but also revealing what was not truth. When Jesus called the disciples, He told them, "I am the way and the truth and the life." (John 14:6a, NABRE) I believe that Holy Spirit protected me. My wife, thanks be to God, called the deacon to help teach me. He taught me the faith and exposed me to the Catholic Church. He catechized me, as we Catholics would say.

I announced to my family that I was going to become a Catholic and I continued my catechism with the deacon. He stayed the course and answered my many questions. He catechized me for two years, and I asked him every question under the sun. He patiently answered everything I came up with during that time.

I understood finally, in my own child-like faith, that I could be forgiven and that God had covered my sin with His own blood. I was being ushered into what I had always thought of as "the white man's" church, but I was learning that it was God's church and race does not matter to God, for God is not a respecter of person.

Then Peter proceeded to speak and said, "In truth, I
see that God shows no partiality."
—Act 10:34, NABRE

I was becoming a Catholic. I started going to some of the prayer meetings, where people were praying in The Spirit (praying in tongues) and laying hands on people in prayer. It was an awesome time!

"The grass withers, the flower wilts,

but the word of our God stands forever."

—Isaiah 40:8, NABRE

GOD'S GRACE:

Reading and studying the Word of God is another essential way that we can grow in our faith. Every time that we open our Bibles, it is a time when God can and will speak to us. Even if we read the same passage every day for a week, that Scripture will speak to us in a different way. The Bible is the Living Word of God.

Bible study cannot be stressed too much. In order to follow God's Will, we must know God's will. St. Jerome said it best, "Ignorance of Scripture is ignorance of Christ." If we want to get to know our Lord and Savior better, then we must read about Him and His life, study what He said and did. Yes, the Christian faith is to be experienced; yet, we must make sure that we are passing on the Truth. If we confess that we believe in Jesus, the Christ and Son of God, then it is important that we know who He is.

Reading the Bible and the Eucharist go hand in hand and they lead to each other—the Bible leads one to the Eucharist and the Eucharist opens up understanding of the Bible. When we read the Scripture at Mass, we are then led to the Eucharist. After Holy Communion, we find that when we read the Scriptures, they are opened for us by the Holy Spirit in a new way and we have new understanding.

CHAPTER THIRTY-TWO
MERCY

LARRY'S STORY:

I was on my journey toward the Catholic Church, toward becoming a Christian, but I wanted to understand what was going to happen with all of my sin. One day I heard this story by a speaker. The man telling the story said that it was a true story.

In the 1700s, there was a great Indian tribe and they were blessed in every regard. They had running water. The Chief was a strong leader. When he spoke, his word became the law, and his law was his word. Everything was going fine, and the tribe's people were thriving and doing well. They had never had any problems. Their enemies did not bother them because they were strong with a strong leader.

Suddenly, there was a problem among the tribe's people; someone was stealing. That had never happened to them before. The Chief, who was a great man, spoke. Whenever he spoke, his word became the law. He said, "When we find that man, we will give him fifty lashes at the hand of the taskmaster." But a strange thing happened; the stealing continued.

Then the Chief again spoke the word that became law, "When we find the thief, we will give him one-hundred lashes at the hand of the taskmaster." One-hundred lashes would kill most men!

One day, they found the thief. The thief turned out to be the mother of the Chief. A great hush fell over the people.

Then the tribe's people said, "Is he going to satisfy his law ..." because when he spoke, his word became the law. "Will he satisfy his law, or will he satisfy his love?"

He loved his mother very much. When the day for the punishment came, they brought the mother of the Chief into the middle of the compound. She was a frail, small woman. They ripped her clothes from her, exposing her back. Then they bound her hand-and-foot in the middle of the compound.

Again, a hush came over the tribe's people. Everyone wondered if he would satisfy his law at the expense of his love.

The Chief raised his hand and the taskmaster came forth with a huge whip in his hand and with bulging muscles, certain to kill the mother of the Chief. The Chief raised his hand and said, "Let the punishment begin." The people could not believe it; the Chief was going to satisfy his law at the expense of his love.

The taskmaster drew back to deliver the first blow, and then the Chief raised his hand again.

Everybody gasped and said, "Oh, he's going to satisfy his love at the expense of his law."

Then the Chief took off his robe and headdress, and handed them to the attendant, exposing his own strong back. He went over to where his mother was bound hand-and-foot in the middle of the compound. He stretched out his arms and he covered his mother with his own body and said, "Let the punishment continue." In that way, he satisfied his law, and his love.

The teller of the story went on to explain that Jesus Christ has covered our sins because the Scripture says in Romans 6:23, "For the wages of sin is death." (NABRE)

I knew that I had been a sinner. But Jesus has covered me with His Body and His own Blood.

In my heart I knew He was saying, *"Father, see my body; see my bloodshed at Calvary for Larry. Don't count his sin against him."* Isaiah 53:5 became clear to me:

"But he was pierced for our sins,

crushed for our iniquity.

He bore the punishment that makes us whole,

by his wounds we were healed."

After that, more of the Scriptures that I read began to make sense. Psalms 103:12 spoke to me, Larry, directly, "I've separated your sin as far as the east is from the west, and I remember it no more." All of these things were beginning to become clearer to me and they began to help me understand what being a child of God meant. That story about God's love and His law had a great influence on my life; it was the beginning of building faith upon faith.

"...from afar the LORD appears:

With age-old love I have loved you;

so I have kept my mercy toward you."

—Jeremiah 31:3, NABRE

GOD'S GRACE:

When we see others getting something good, sometimes it can be hard to be happy for them and not upset for ourselves. Sometimes we just cannot understand why certain things seem to happen to us versus someone else or no one at all. Why do bad things happen? Many times, we choose to blame God—perhaps we feel safe blaming God because in the back of our minds, we know that God will still love us. But even when bad things do happen, God can bring great things from the bad. He can redeem any situation.

"We know that all things work for good for those who love God, who are called according to his purpose."
—Romans 8:28, NABRE

CHAPTER THIRTY-THREE
BAPTISM

LARRY'S STORY:

I came into the Catholic Church and became a Christian when I was twenty-seven. People often ask, "What did you convert from?" but I had no previous formal religious affiliation. I had never been baptized. Although my mom had a Baptist background, I was not a Baptist. I was not trained in the Baptist faith except for the brief experience of church that I had as a young boy on the mourning bench. I cannot say that I converted from anything. I like to say that I was just a 'regular heathen.'

I felt like I was caught up in something special; everything was new. Everything Catholic was wonderful. My only experience had been the mourning bench on Way Way Plantation. I shared with my brother James that I was going to become a Catholic. James, at this point, was not very churched himself. Neither were my other brothers. Later, two of them would become ordained ministers. I was going down to The Bayou to be baptized and to receive my First Holy Communion.

As an adult Catholic, I believe that I was one of the first black adults ever baptized in Our Lady of the Rosary Church on Bayou Lafourche. Lafourche is French for "fork." The ironic symbolism dramatically describes my life changing directional shift. This indeed was the *fork* in the road of my life.

The church was full. My mom was there. My brother George (who is now a Baptist minister) was there. Mom had previously said to the deacon who had catechized me and was going to baptize me, "Look, I understand Larry's going to be a Catholic, but I want to make sure that he goes under the water. I don't want just sprinkling for my boy, even if he's going to be a Catholic." So the deacon arranged for a large tub of water for me to be immersed in to satisfy my mother.

I was emotional, but calm. I was filled up to over-flowing. Everything was beautiful, and everything was set. They had a white robe for me to put on for the Sacrament of Baptism; I do not even remember where the white robe came from. I had previously met many of the people of the Catholic charismatic community on the Bayou because I had been to their prayer meetings. They all showed up to welcome me into the church; it was a beautiful thing.

I went down in the water with no fear. I was anticipating. I was overjoyed. I was filled up with God's love, His mercy, and His peace. I could not believe that I was being ushered into this great mystery of faith, of God, and of His people. My heart was spilling over with love.

I could hardly believe that all of the hate-filled thoughts that I had embraced in my past were now somehow separated from me. Calling white people "blue-eyed devils," wanting to take up arms, join the Black Panther Party, and kill people, it was all gone. Being happy when Mark Essex was shooting at white people from the Howard Johnson Hotel in New Orleans was gone. All of that was swept away.

All of the indignity I had suffered as a young man disappeared as well. All the pain of seeing my family struggle for so many years and enduring the end of the Jim Crow Laws was gone. All of the humiliation in high school from a seemingly racist principal and teachers had vanished. My hatred of the people who threw the coke bottles, eggs, and garbage at me and my brothers while we waited for the bus after cutting their grass had been swept away.

I came out of the Baptismal waters, and literally, my parents, my brothers, and all of the white people there looked like they had the faces of angels. Everyone looked bright with light and beauty. Beaming. Wonderful. Peaceful.

> "Call to me, and I will answer you; I will tell you great things
> beyond the reach of your knowledge."
> —Jeremiah 33:3, NABRE

GOD'S GRACE:

The Sacrament of Baptism is one of the seven sacraments of the Catholic Church. The seven sacraments in the Church are: Baptism, Confirmation, Eucharist, Reconciliation, Anointing of the Sick, Holy Orders, and Matrimony. *The Catechism of the Catholic Church* teaches:

> The sacraments are efficacious signs of grace, instituted by Christ and entrusted to the Church, by which divine life is dispensed to us. The visible rites by which the sacraments are celebrated signify and make present the graces proper to each sacrament... (*CCC* 1131)

When one asks to join the Catholic Church they are expressing a desire to join the Church. The Church has a program called RCIA (Rite of Christian Initiation) for a person to go through to make sure that a person has an opportunity to learn about the Church and what it teaches. If a person chooses to be baptized, then he/she is saying that they are in agreement with what the Church teaches and that he/she will be submitted to the Church's authority. Joining the Church is done through the Sacraments of Baptism, Confirmation, and receiving First Eucharist.

CHAPTER THIRTY-FOUR
THE EUCHARIST

LARRY'S STORY:

The first time the Body of Christ was on my tongue, I was caught up in something eternal. It felt like a dream. It was almost unbelievable that God had caught me up, and I was a part of this great Church. I knew without a doubt that this really was God's true Church, His true Communion.

I could not believe that I was actually receiving Holy Communion. It was more than a dream; it was my destiny. During the whole preparation for my baptism, it was like I was awake, but I was half-asleep. It was surreal.

"I know someone in Christ who, fourteen years ago (whether in the body or out of the body I do not know, God knows), was caught up to the third heaven."
—2 Corinthians 12:2, NABRE

St. Paul is writing about how someone was not sure if he was in heaven or if he was on earth when he was caught up to the third heaven. I was just caught up. I was just caught up in this whole beauty of Holy Communion, and receiving the Body of Christ.

I can still hear the music that was playing when Holy Communion was being distributed, "I Am the Bread of Life." I was eating the Bread of Life, I was eating Jesus Christ, the Eucharist, and He tasted sweet and beautiful.

Now I understand fully that I am not participating in any cannibalism. My mind and my heart both finally came to that realization. I know that I am participating in the greatest gift; I am entering into the same sacrifice that Jesus made at Calvary. I know I am not re-sacrificing Jesus because Scripture teaches that one sacrifice has been made by Jesus Christ; there is no need to kill Him again. He has already been slain. The Lamb has been slain, the Lamb has risen, and the Lamb will come again. (See 1 Corinthians 11:23-29; Mark 14:22-24; Matthew 26:26-28; Luke 22:19-20; John 6:51-56; 1 Corinthians 5:7; and Hebrews 10:12 below.)

> For I received from the Lord what I also handed on to you, that the Lord Jesus, on the night he was handed over, took bread, and, after he had given thanks, broke it and said, "This is my body that is for you. Do this in remembrance of me." In the same way also the cup, after supper, saying, "This cup is the new covenant in my blood. Do this, as often as you drink it, in remembrance of me." For as often as you

eat this bread and drink the cup, you proclaim the death of the Lord until he comes.

Therefore whoever eats the bread or drinks the cup of the Lord unworthily will have to answer for the body and blood of the Lord. A person should examine himself, and so eat the bread and drink the cup. For anyone who eats and drinks without discerning the body, eats and drinks judgment on himself.
—1 Corinthians 11:23-29, NABRE

While they were eating, he took bread, said the blessing, broke it, and gave it to them, and said, "Take it; this is my body." Then he took a cup, gave thanks, and gave it to them, and they all drank from it. He said to them, "This is my blood of the covenant, which will be shed for many.
—Mark 14:22-24, NABRE

While they were eating, Jesus took bread, said the blessing, broke it, and giving it to his disciples said, "Take and eat; this is my body." Then he took a cup, gave thanks, and gave it to them, saying, "Drink from it, all of you, for this is my blood of the covenant, which will be shed on behalf of many for the forgiveness of sins.
—Matthew 26:26-28, NABRE

Then he took the bread, said the blessing, broke it, and gave it to them, saying, "This is my body, which will be given for you; do this in memory of me." And likewise the cup after they had eaten, saying, "This cup is the new covenant in my blood, which will be shed for you.
—Luke 22:19-20, NABRE

I am the living bread that came down from heaven; whoever eats this bread will live forever; and the bread that I will give is my flesh for the life of the world." The Jews quarreled among themselves, saying, "How can this man give us [his] flesh to eat?" Jesus said to them, "Amen, amen, I say to you, unless you eat the flesh of the Son of Man and drink his blood, you do not have life within you. Whoever eats my flesh and drinks my blood has eternal life, and I will raise him on the last day. For my flesh is true food, and my blood is true drink. Whoever eats my flesh and drinks my blood remains in me and I in him.
—John 6:51-56, NABRE

Clear out the old yeast, so that you may become a fresh batch of dough, inasmuch as you are unleavened. For our paschal lamb, Christ, has been sacrificed.
—1 Corinthians 5:7, NABRE

But this one offered one sacrifice for sins, and took his seat forever at the right hand of God.
—Hebrews 10:12, NABRE

God's amazing grace was helping me to overcome the power of race and had ushered me into the Church of the living God. I received the Sacraments of Baptism, First Communion, and Confirmation, all during one Mass. It was an awesome thing!

When I first received the Eucharist, the Body of Christ on my tongue, in my hands, words cannot describe the consuming presence of God that I experienced. Words cannot properly detail how awesome it is to behold the Lamb of God who took away my sins. Going to Holy Communion, even now, is still an amazing, humbling, and overwhelming act.

"Amen, amen, I say to you, whoever believes has eternal life. I am the bread of life. Your ancestors ate the manna in the desert, but they died; this is the bread that comes down from heaven so that one may eat it and not die. I am the living bread that came down from heaven; whoever eats this bread will live forever; and the bread that I will give is my flesh for the life of the world."
—John 6:47-51, NABRE

GOD'S GRACE:

The Eucharist is received during Holy Communion. Catholics believe that the Eucharist is the Body and Blood, Soul and Divinity of our Lord Jesus Christ. We call the Eucharistic meal Holy Communion, "because by this sacrament we unite ourselves to Christ, who makes us sharers in his Body and Blood to form a single body." (*CCC* 1331)

CHAPTER THIRTY-FIVE
HOLY SPIRIT

LARRY'S STORY:

After I was Baptized, there was an anointing, a fire from the Holy Spirit that rested upon me. I had never experienced anything like that before. It was like the dove of the Holy Spirit was over me; and He was powerful but gentle, and yet a strong presence. The only word that I can use to describe it is the "anointing."

"But you have the anointing that comes from the holy one, and you all have knowledge."
—1 John 2:20

"But the one who gives us security with you in Christ and who anointed us is God; he has also put his seal upon us and given the Spirit in our hearts as a first installment."
—2 Corinthians 1:21-22

I am using that word (anointing), looking forward, because I certainly did not know what it meant then. I had heard about it though never experienced it. I felt like I was swallowed up in the glory of God. There was a sense of God's holiness, a sense of His presence, a sense that I was now in God and God was now in me.

The anointing was heavy and overpowering. The heavy anointing remained with me for three or four days. It was not like something took me over. When I was awake, I was aware of the presence of The Spirit. I looked at the people that I encountered in a new way; I had a new compassion in me. I think it had already started, but Baptism, First Communion, and Confirmation sealed if for me.

I was a new person. I was a new creation. I knew that's what the Scripture said, but I could feel the sensations of change. I felt myself become a new and altered person after I came out of the water and had received Holy Communion for the first time. After I was confirmed in the Church, I was a different person. The old Larry was gone. I knew that I was a new being just like 2 Corinthians 5:17 describes: "So whoever is in Christ is a new creation: the old things have passed away; behold, new things have come." (NABRE) I was experiencing a newness of life. Old things truly had passed away and everything was genuinely new.

I knew a man named Jimmy, a lawyer that worked for the same company that I worked for. When I came back from that Thursday night service, he brought me a little gift and a card, just welcoming me to the Church. He was a Catholic with a big family. Jimmy was the first person outside of my family to welcome me into the Body of Christ at my workplace. It was just an awesome time in my life.

A friend named Bob and I were co-workers and Bob was caught up in my Baptism. He had been a cradle-Catholic (a Catholic who was baptized as an infant and raised in the faith), but now he and I would go to the mall and look for people to tell about Jesus. We were on fire for God. I was on fire, and Bob's faith was rekindled while experiencing my conversion process with me. There was an overflow of God's love; then there was an afterglow after the Baptism.

I went to work with the sensation of newness. God's atmosphere of love thoroughly encompassed me. It was an overwhelming, heavy awareness of the presence of God and sensing His presence in my life and in my actions, my words, and my dealings with people. It is very difficult to explain; but those that have encountered it, know it.

This anointing of the Holy Spirit, this fire of God's love is something that is experiential. It is called, "the baptism of the Holy Spirit." (To learn more on the baptism of the Holy Spirit, please see: *Baptism in the Holy Spirit* by International Catholic Charismatic Renewal Services.)

I had experienced that, and was still feeling it. What I did not know was that I could experience this baptism in the Holy Spirit more than once. This is not the same as being baptized with water. This is the outpouring of the Holy Spirit that I received right after being baptized at Confirmation. It is a fresh outpouring of The Spirit, an infilling.

It is said that there is one Baptism, but there are many "fillings." I was experiencing just one of the fillings of The Spirit. Once you are baptized, you receive the indwelling Holy Spirit permanently; however, a person can receive an infilling more than once.

I was experiencing the infilling. I already had the indwelling at Baptism; but I was now experiencing the infilling and the overflow. I have experienced it many times since. It is not a hyper-emotional experience like many people think. It is vast, deep, wide, and weighty. It is the glory of God being made manifest or showing forth in a person's life and they are aware of it. It is God's presence with us, in us, and around us.

"Now the Lord is the Spirit, and where the Spirit of the Lord
is, there is freedom."
—2 Corinthians 3:17, NABRE

GOD'S GRACE:

The Holy Spirit is the Third Person of the Holy Trinity. *The Catechism of the Catholic Church* teaches:

> "Holy Spirit" is the proper name of the one whom we adore and glorify with the Father and the Son. The Church has received this name from the Lord and professes it in the Baptism of her new children.

> …On the other hand, "Spirit" and "Holy" are divine attributes common to the three divine persons. By joining the two terms, Scripture, liturgy, and theological language designate the inexpressible person of the Holy Spirit, without any possible equivocation with other uses of the terms "spirit" and "holy." (*CCC* 691)

CHAPTER THIRTY-SIX
LEARNING MORE

LARRY'S STORY:

I left the insurance company that I was working for and I went to work for another insurance company that offered me a substantial raise if I would come and work for them. I couldn't refuse the offer. I worked for them for almost four years in the Metairie (New Orleans area). They soon offered me a job at several places around the country; one of them was in Seattle. I took the job in Seattle as Regional Manager over Alaska, Seattle, Idaho, and Oregon. My entire staff was white. It was a different situation in Seattle; generally the people were very kind. There did not seem to be any blatant racism like I had experienced down south.

We prayed about whether we should move to Seattle. However, as I remember now, God never really answered. He never said, "Go." I learned a valuable lesson there; nevertheless it all worked out. God did not say, "Go."   I went because He wasn't saying

"No." I asked my deacon friend to pray with us. He said, "Well, you know, He's going to tell you what to do." I did not really understand what that meant at the time. I now know that when you ask God a question, you should wait for an answer.

My career in Seattle was going well. During the four plus years that I was there, I had a great staff, earned good bonuses, had a boat, two cars, a large house in a great neighborhood. Our children were attending a very good school.

We were actively involved in the Western Washington Catholic Charismatic Renewal in the area and we had friends in the community who readily accepted us. From my perspective the move to Seattle was a success. My wife never fully adjusted to Seattle and the weather there, so we made a decision to move back to Louisiana.

The priest visited our house, and we had friends in the community who readily accepted us. We actually purchased the same house we used to live in. One cannot recreate the past. Things are never the same as they once were. It was a difficult transition time for our family. We stayed in that house for less than a year, and then moved to the area that where I currently live.

I continued to learn about my faith. The deacon that had taught me now had become more than just the one who was helping to form me and teach me the faith. He was becoming my friend.

> "We know that all things work for good for those who love God,
> who are called according to his purpose."
> —Romans 8:28, NABRE

GOD'S GRACE:

We have a tendency to want things NOW. Our culture constantly feeds into this by offering us fast food, movies on demand, and other seemingly quick fixes to our needs. Prayer is different. When we pray and ask the Lord for help, we need to be prepared to wait patiently for an answer. Sometimes the answer may come quickly and we can act on God's answer. At other times, the answer may take time. There can be many reasons for this, but the bottom line is that we need to learn to wait on the Lord. God's timing is not always what our schedule would desire; however, He sees more than we do and He knows what is best for us.

CHAPTER THIRTY-SEVEN
FORGIVENESS

LARRY'S STORY:

As I began to allow the Holy Spirit to move in my life, God began to deal with many of my past issues that had affected and shaped my life. I wanted to confront my dad about his not taking care of our family, so I went to find him so that I could speak to him. I found him back in the country, on the plantation. When I asked him questions, I chose my words carefully, trying not to be disrespectful. I didn't want to start a fight, but just wanted to get answers so I could understand his absence and apparent lack of support.

My dad pulled out a little box of money order receipts that he had saved for fifteen years or more. I guess he knew that one day one of his children was going to ask him about these things once we were adults. He showed me that he had sent money orders of ten dollars, fifteen dollars, five dollars, every week to my mom to support our large family as best as he could. His attitude was one of wanting to give answers to all my questions, perhaps because I presented myself humbly to him.

I came in tears to him. "Dad I want to understand. Mom says that you did not do enough for the family. Why didn't you send more? You knew we were struggling in the city. Why didn't you come and visit us?" I just wanted to know.

When God starts to move in your heart, you want to know the truth. Whether it is hard or ugly or painful, you just want truth because "the truth will set you free," according to John 8:32 (NABRE).

When I told him that we did a lot of fishing down near New Orleans, he asked me if I wanted to go fishing. The next thing I knew, we were fishing. For the first time in my life, I went fishing with my father. I remember very clearly that we went over the levy to the outlets from Lake Providence and he had a boat, a flat boat in the back of his truck.

I was impressed that my dad was so strong at his age. He asked me if I could help him to pull the boat out of the truck, and I nodded. He laughed when I asked him if he had a pair of gloves. He just laughed at me. My dad was always a hard worker, and he was used to doing things with his hands.

"Don't worry about it son, I've got it." And he pulled the boat out of the truck by himself.

My dad treated me well, and in fact, we always shared a sense of reconciliation after that incident. I never regretted going and finding him and learning his explanation. I cried with him. We cried with one another. I never knew him like this. I had a father; he was imperfect, but I was so happy to get to know him.

I was never old enough to talk to my dad before he dropped out of my life. I was a child when we moved from the plantation. Children did not speak to their parents with familiarity when I grew up. That was considered disrespectful. But now, I was back on Way Way Plantation, and I was talking to my dad. We talked like two men, not father and son.

We only caught two little fish but it did not matter because I was in the boat with my dad. I could tell by the way he cast and the way he steered the boat and studied the water that my dad was a good fisherman. There was an alligator swimming around in the area where we were. He was not afraid. He told me, "That ol' alligator is not going to do anything."

I just felt safe with my dad, even as a twenty-eight year old. I was not worried. We did not have any life jackets in the boat or anything, I don't swim, and that water was deep but I was not worried—I was with my father.

That visit cleared up all of my questions in regards to my dad. My dad did not act frustrated with me for asking so many personal things. He did not even seem to mind telling me things that I had no business asking. We talked all day and then I stayed for a second day. It was a wonderful time.

Back on Way Way Plantation, working for the property owner, my father gave his whole life to that land. He just wore out from driving the tractors, working with the chemicals, and then having an injury on the job. He underwent back surgery as a result and it turned out pretty bad. The healthcare was lacking and he suffered for it.

I never went fishing with him again, and never will, since he passed away last year. Nevertheless, I have that memory solid in my mind. Dad and I bonded on that flat boat. I headed home with an overflowing heart of love for my dad. He was buried on the Plantation, but land can no longer hold him—he is now free because he died in faith.

Dad died in the summer of 2011. I had the privilege to share these words at his funeral: "There was a man named Job that had 7,000 sheep, 3,000 camels, 500 teams of oxen and 500 female donkeys. Job was rich! Upon his death my dad had no sheep, no camels, no oxen and no female donkeys. By all outward appearances my dad was poor. Yet, he died rich! He had thirteen sons, nine daughters, scores of grandchildren and great grandchildren. Through his loins came three ordained ministers, a Catholic, a Baptist and a Pentecostal, two deacons and one faithful wife who cared for him in his frailty toward the end of his life.

"Three events about dad stand out in my memory. One was when he came home early and caught us boys playing cards on top of the freezer. He did not want us playing cards and when he caught us it was not a pretty sight especially when he went to the tree to break off a limb (not a branch) to give out the punishment. I have many reasons to not be able to forget him in that moment. The second memory was of the one and only time that I got to go fishing behind the levee with him. It was a father/son moment that I will treasure forever. Despite the fact that we only caught two small fish during that brief time together, the time allowed us to catch something much bigger and longer lasting. I saw my dad as a father with his son. The final memory was of my dad being baptized in the lake. He looked so serene as he approached and went down into the water! It was a great day for him and a great day for our family to see him come to faith in Jesus Christ. My mother was very happy for my dad and she also attended his baptism, even though they had been estranged for many years.

"Dad, you gave your whole life to the land and now you will be buried on the land that you worked. Even though you will be buried there, neither the land nor its owners has a hold on you anymore. You are free now Clifton, Bubba, dad. Your struggle is over and the Lord himself is extending his hand to you and saying, "Come now and enjoy all I have prepared for you. Come now, take up your rest in the 'new land'.""

"If you forgive others their transgressions, your heavenly Father will
forgive you."
— Matthew 6:14, NABRE

GOD'S GRACE:

Jesus taught about forgiveness many times. It is crucial that Christians forgive—not just other Christians, but everyone. Without forgiveness, we can become bitter and bitterness leads to other sins. When we forgive someone, we are acknowledging that he or she has hurt us and that we are choosing to forgive that person. It does not mean that what that person did was right or alright to do; it just means that we are choosing to not hold that sin against the person.

In the case of parents, it can be doubly devastating when they let a child down. As a parent, a person is supposed to take care of his/her child. But even parents are human and they make mistakes. There is a Scripture about noticing a splinter in someone else's eye while one has a wooden beam in his own:

"Why do you notice the splinter in your brother's eye, but do not perceive the wooden beam in your own eye?"
—Matthew 7:3

Although this Scripture is usually used to teach about being a hypocrite, it can also be used to talk about forgiveness. We want God to forgive the "wooden beam" in our eyes, but it is important that we forgive the "splinter" of someone else. Splinters can hurt, especially when they are from our family members. The only way to pull them out is by truly forgiving the person.

CHAPTER THIRTY-EIGHT
THE WORD OF GOD

LARRY'S STORY:

I love the Word of God—Old Testament and New Testament. I love studying the Word of God; I love everything about the Scriptures. I love the Eucharist. I am a Catholic, I believe, because of the Eucharist; it drew me to the Church. What once had dissuaded me from entering into God had now pulled me into Him.

I got deeper into the faith. I was teaching from the Scriptures about a year after I was baptized. Someone asked me to teach a Bible study and I did. I began giving my testimony and teaching at a prayer meeting at the age of twenty-eight. I will not say I barely knew the Scriptures. I had gotten a lot of catechesis, a lot of teaching. I was reading many books and listening to others teach. I found it somewhat shocking that at that time many Catholics did not really know much about the Bible.

It was really surprising that grown people who had been faithful people for many years did not know anything about the Scripture. They seemed to know little about the promises of God, little about healing, or to even believe that evil was real.

Naturally, I had an inclination towards teaching; I always wanted to be a teacher, so it was not hard for me to begin to study the Scriptures in earnest, rather than just read the Bible. I was teaching the best psychology known to mankind—the love of God.

A cradle-Catholic is someone who was baptized as a child (usually a couple of weeks after birth). I would never call myself a preacher, or a person that preached. As a young country boy, a man that lived near our house on the plantation nicknamed me *Preacher*. He called me *Preacher* because I would stand on a stump and curse like a sailor in a litany of curses. He said, "That boy's gonna be a preacher." Don't ask me how he came to this conclusion.

The more I studied God's Word the stronger my desire for the Word grew. A priest friend who saw my desire gave me a concordance. This helped me to study even more. Hebrews 4:12 says, "The word of God is living and effective." (NABRE) The power of God's Word was holding me close to Him and teaching me of His wonderfulness. This was back before we had all that information available on the internet. I still have that concordance.

My wife and I went to the pastor of the church that we were attending. We spoke about the fact that we felt the church needed more.

He simply nodded and said, "Yeah, I know, so what are you going to do about it?"

That is what he said! I was dumbfounded. So we started a prayer group with one of the nuns at Holy Rosary Dominican Retreat Center, the priest, and my wife and I; just the four of us started the first charismatic prayer group there.

Exposed to the Catholic charismatic environment, I attended many meetings and charismatic masses at *The Center of Jesus the Lord*, a parish in New Orleans led by Father Emile LaFrance. This Catholic charismatic parish, right on the edge of the French Quarter, ministers in the powerful gifts of the Holy Spirit. I thought that all Catholics were charismatic. I quickly realized that there was one part of the Church that was charismatic while other parts were not as open to the charismatic perspective. To be charismatic in the Catholic Church means that one allows the Holy Spirit, given at Baptism, and again poured out during Confirmation, to work in and through oneself. (There are probably many Catholics who do experience the gifts of the Holy Spirit but would not necessarily call themselves charismatics.) Charismatics are also open to the "charismatic" spiritual gifts, as St. Paul teaches in 1 Corinthians (and other Scriptures): the gift of tongues, interpretation, prophecy, miracles, healing, etc.

"Heaven and earth will pass away, but my words will not pass away."
— Mark 13:31, NABRE

GOD'S GRACE:

There is Bible reading and Bible study. These are two different things, but both are imperative to a strong Christian walk. Bible reading is reading the Bible for knowledge, wisdom, Truth, and enjoyment. When we do Bible study however, we are looking at what the Bible is really saying, putting it into the context of where and when it was being said and to whom, as well as deciding what impact it will have on our lives. Bible reading can be done anywhere and at any time to help a person grow in his/her knowledge and understanding of God and the things of God.

Bible study can be done with the aid of a Bible with commentary notes, *The Catechism of the Catholic Church*, a theological dictionary, and other study tools (like a Bible study guide). Before we begin either Bible reading or Bible study, we should pray and ask the Holy Spirit to help us to understand the Scriptures.

CHAPTER THIRTY-NINE
ANSWERING THE CALL

LARRY'S STORY:

Three to four years after coming into the church, at thirty-one years old, with four children, I was beginning to feel a call to the diaconate (to be an ordained deacon in the Catholic Church). I inquired about the diaconate, an ordained ministry in the Church; however, the Church's response was that I was too young to be a deacon. You cannot be ordained. You have to be thirty-five before you can be accepted in the diaconate formation program.

I was totally disappointed and somewhat confused about that. I did not understand it at that time. It was not until I was thirty-nine-years old that I inquired again, and then I was accepted into the diaconate program.

While I was in training for the diaconate, I was given permission to teach at a men's conference in Clarksdale with a friend, Deacon Alex Jones, a black ordained Catholic deacon from the Diocese of Detroit (a converted Pentecostal minister who brought fifty members to the Catholic Church). We had someone driving us and it allowed us to focus and converse without thought for the road. We were on this journey to Clarksdale, and we looked at one another and realized, twenty, thirty years ago, we would not be traveling through Mississippi to preach at a white Catholic Church as the two principal teachers and speakers.

It hit us how good God is, and how Mississippi was once a desert for me and now I was one of the people that was bringing the water of the Word back to the desert that I had been afraid of before. Who can do something like that, except God?

In order to be accepted as a deacon, one's wife has to write a letter saying that she accepts that her husband is going to be an ordained person, and that he is going to be a member of the clergy as a deacon. As a deacon, one of the things one has to commit to is that if his wife dies he agrees that he is not going to remarry. If I had been ordained a deacon, and if my wife divorced me, my only option was going to be a celibate deacon (I could not remarry), and that is the same case now.

I was three plus years into the diaconate program at Notre Dame Seminary when my wife asked for a divorce. I was about a year and a half from being ordained. The divorce was hard to go through. I was in the desert. The only thing I had was God. You have your family, but they do not really understand. It was a struggle I had to go through alone. My close secular friends suggested that I start dating. They meant well, but that was not what I needed or what I was looking for at that time. I would go to the prayer meetings (because the prayer meetings still went on) and those meetings were a great support to me.

God is merciful. If I had been married before I was ordained, I would not have been able to marry again. My state in life would have been a celibate deacon, and I would not have had a wife. There is a Scripture that says, "…for it is better to marry than to be on fire." (1 Corinthians 7:9b, NABRE) Some need to marry; I think I am one of those people.

"Commit your way to the LORD;

trust in him and he will act."

— Psalm 37:5, NABRE

GOD'S GRACE:

What does it mean to be "called?" When we are called by God into something, like a ministry, it means that we feel that the Lord is directing us to begin a new endeavor. Being called to something doesn't mean that it will happen overnight; we still have to put in the time, energy, and effort into training and learning the ministry.

One of the most helpful phrases concerning being called is: *God doesn't call the qualified, He qualifies the called.* This is a key point to keep in mind if you think that God is calling you into a ministry and you are wondering: *how, when, where, who,* or *how much.* Yes, we have to put in the time and commitment; however, it is by God's strength and resources that we accomplish our goals when we are called into ministry.

Another key to accepting a call from God is that we have to be willing to accept the authority already in place—beginning with God, all the way through to the person that is currently leading the ministry that we are going to join. Many people are willing to accept God's authority and even the Church's authority, but they struggle when it comes to accepting the authority of those who are currently in charge. God is a God of order, and showing that we can obey authority is important. Displaying that we have a teachable spirit is also essential to the success of our new calling.

CHAPTER FORTY
GOD'S PLAN

LARRY'S STORY:

God has our lives so intimately planned. Ten years earlier, I knew a certain woman at church but I never knew she had a daughter. I had no idea this woman would ultimately become my mother-in-law. After I met her beautiful daughter in church, things slowly progressed and we began dating. I really was not looking for anyone. I was doing ministry at the time. We met at her church.

While we were dating, we had many serious discussions. Neither of us wanted anything but a solid, faith-filled partner. She was strong in her faith and I was striving to be a man of God.

She was a teacher with a Master's in Education and Supervision. She does not teach today. She plans to go back and get a Master's in Divinity or in Scripture one day. She is a beautiful woman with a striking, quiet spirit. My children love her; they are respectful to her. She is a good, solid person. We have one son together. We will be married eleven years this June (2012).

In order to be a deacon in the Catholic Church, one had to be married for at least five years, so I continued to learn and grow in my faith. In 2008, I spoke to the Archbishop. He accepted me back into the diaconate program and I was ordained as a Deacon at St. Louis King of France Cathedral in New Orleans on December 13, 2008. My ordination was very emotional for me. I recall all that I had been through in experiencing God's amazing grace. Here I was in a city that at one time held over a hundred thousand slaves less than two miles away (in Congo Square) from where I was ordained. In that same city, the Archbishop laid his hands on me in prayer, very close to where my ancestors were held as slaves.

I was later assigned to St. Louis Cathedral, in the famous French Quarter, to read the Gospel and preach the Word of God. I am also assigned to a predominantly black Catholic church, Our Lady of Grace Parish in Reserve, Louisiana, which is situated on the Mississippi River (the Spanish referred to the Mississippi River at the river of the Holy Spirit).

"Find your delight in the LORD

who will give you your heart's desire."

— Psalm 37:4, NABRE

GOD'S GRACE:

One way to grow in your spiritual life is to have a strong awareness of God. Noticing that God is present in our lives is one method of doing this. As we begin to see the movements of God in our lives, we need to start "stepping" into them through agreement prayer. Praying in agreement with God is essential.

This type of prayer allows a person to state what he/she believes God is doing in his/her life, what God wants to do in his/her life, and then agree with God that we want to help with that movement. One type of agreement prayer that is communal as well as individual is the *Our Father Prayer*. When we pray this prayer, we say, "Thy Kingdom come, Thy will be done." It is God's will that we are praying to be accomplished, not our own. We pray to bring that Kingdom reality to earth.

CHAPTER FORTY-ONE
NOT THE END

LARRY'S STORY:

My mom knew a lot sooner than I did that I was called to ministry. Apparently, several people in my family knew it. My older brother, Cliff, and my brother George knew it. From what they have shared with me, they thought I had a calling on my life to preach the Word of God. They are not Catholic; one is an ordained Pentecostal minister, and the other is an ordained Southern Baptist minister. They respect the knowledge of the Scriptures in me. They respect my ministry, and I respect theirs.

Mom did not actually make it to the ordination, but she came to my first Mass. Five months after I was ordained, my mother died. At her funeral, they sang, "I'll Fly Away," (but "I Fly Away" for me). It was truly what is known in the black Baptist Church as a 'home going.'

It was a beautiful thing to see: black people, white people, and her large family all together. It was an amazing thing. We celebrated her life, and the gift that she was to us. She was a faith-filled woman. She was a great cook. She ministered to all of her daughters-in-law in the family. She taught my wife how to make her special gumbo. She was an all-around good woman. So many young women were naturally attracted to her goodness. In addition, many young men like my nephews went to her for counsel. She was always an encourager.

Whenever I was having a rough time, or struggling with some issue, I would go and sit in the simple little house where she lived and she would always say, "It's gonna be alright son."

Just that effortless word of faith, which was part of her ministry, comforted me and countless others. Mom always had a word of faith. That was my mom. She was a strong woman—emotionally and spiritually.

Well over a thousand people came to her funeral. The small Baptist church was filled to overflowing. My mother, Beatrice, had lots of friends and family. Mom never drove a car, but she managed to touch people's lives, literally, all over the country.

I fondly remember Mom's 75th birthday. The entire family was gathered to honor her on this evening. I had the honor of being the MC to keep things going. Mom had a way of making everyone want to be around her and of course everyone was invited. I do mean everyone. The in-laws, former in-laws, former spouses of children, neighbors and many other people that she had touched with her life were there. Many stood and gave witness to how she had touched their lives over the many years despite her apparent limitation of education and financial resources. They testified about how mom had quietly given food when she had little herself, how she had encouraged someone who had troubles. Mom was an encourager and a fighter! She had a humble dignity about her and when she shared about her struggles with her voice trembling I was moved by the power of the spirit of perseverance and faith that the Lord had given her.

We were all gathered around, listening intently to her every word. There was no doubt the Lord had protected and provided for her and her family and many others that he had sent into her life. We knew then that we would not have mom in our midst for too many more years, but that evening she was with us and the power of God's grace pressing down on her and into her life was a powerful witness to everyone within the sound of her voice and in her presence.

"Blessed are they who mourn,

for they will be comforted."

— Matthew 5:4, NABRE

GOD'S GRACE:

The importance of having a spiritual mentor cannot be stressed enough. A spiritual mentor is someone who has been on a similar faith-journey as you and can help you walk your own journey of faith. I say "similar faith-journey" because everyone is different and the way God communicates with each of us will therefore be different. The way in which we perceive God and react to God will be different as well.

A mentor does not need to have gone through every experience to be a mentor. Nor does a mentor need to be older than you are. A good mentor is someone with the gift of encouragement. A few things to look for in a good mentor are: that they have similar spiritual gifts as you, they lead a Spirit-filled life, they want to be a mentor, and they feel that they are called to be a mentor to you at this time.

A good spiritual mentor is someone who will encourage us to step out in faith, to answer the call of God on our lives, and be there for us as a spiritual authority in the area that they are helping us to grow in at this time. Spiritual mentors usually have a "season" that they help us and then we may change to another mentor for a different season. God sends people into our lives—throughout our lives—that are meant to encourage, guide, teach, train, gently correct, and to mentor us in our spiritual growth.

CHAPTER FORTY-TWO
JUSTICE AND MERCY

LARRY'S STORY:

As a young man, I wanted justice. However, I wanted justice the way that human beings look at it. I heard a young preacher teach about mercy and justice. "Mercy is greater than justice," he said. The great Indian Chief story and this story about Mercy and Justice are two great stories that showed me God's great love for us. Mercy is indeed greater than justice!

The story goes:

Justice said to Mercy, "Let's have a meeting at three o'clock at Jacob's well. Don't you be late."

Mercy said, "Don't worry Justice; I'll be there right on time."

So Justice got to Jacob's well first, and he was walking around the well. Suddenly, Justice became stuck in quicksand. (See, sometimes Justice gets stuck). *Justice was going down for the count; he was up to his knees, then up to his waist, and then up to his neck.*

The more he struggled, the deeper he got. Justice was going down in the quicksand and about to be snuffed out. He cried out, "Oh Mercy, where art thou?"

Mercy was nowhere to be seen. One last time, he cried out, "Oh Mercy!"

Suddenly, Justice felt the hand of Mercy on his hand. Mercy pulled Justice out of the quicksand. Justice got out of the quicksand, washed himself off, and said, "Mercy, where were you when I called out to you?"

Mercy said, "Oh Justice, I heard you calling out to me. I was on my way to help you and I heard my friends, Shadrach, Meshach, and Abednego. They were in the fiery furnace, and I had to get in that fiery furnace and fan the flames. I'm sorry that I smell like smoke, but I had to help those three Jewish boys.

When I heard you cry out, I was on my way to help you, and then I heard my friend, Daniel, in the lion's den. And ol' Mercy had to get in the lion's den and close up the mouth of the lion. I'm sorry that my clothes are a little bit torn.

Finally, I was on my way to help you, and then I heard Moses. He was down at the Red Sea backed up against the wall. The Egyptians were hot on his trail. I went down to the Red Sea and fanned the waves with the other side of my garment, and I caused a wall of water to stand on either side of them so they could pass through on dry land. I'm sorry; I got a little bit wet.

Then I heard your cry, and I got on the wings of Goodness and Kindness, and flew quickly and came here and pulled you out of the quicksand. Justice said, "I see how it is with you, Mercy. You may not come when I want you to, but you are always right on time."

That showed me, that yes, I was demanding justice as a young, angry black man. But God's mercy is indeed greater than justice. I understood when I heard that story. God was building precept upon precept for me, truth upon truth with the Indian Chief and with the story of Justice and Mercy. Those are a part of me now. They will forever be a part of me.

I minister in a city where at the height of the slave trade in the 1700s, it held more slaves than any other city in United States. It was a normal thing to find up to a hundred thousand slaves in the city of New Orleans, in Congo Square at any one time. It is an open space within Louis Armstrong Park, in the Tremé neighborhood, just across Rampart Street and north of the French Quarter. Moreover, a third of the slaves were women and children. I have to pass right by Congo Square every time I leave the Cathedral. The memories of a past I was not part of echoes in my thinking when I come near that section of the city. It is very powerful!

"For sin is not to have any power over you, since you are not under the law but under grace."
— Romans 6:14, NABRE

GOD'S GRACE:

God is merciful and just. Scripture teaches us:

What then are we to say? Is there injustice on the part of God? Of course not! For he says to Moses:

"I will show mercy to whom I will,

I will take pity on whom I will."

So it depends not upon a person's will or exertion, but upon God, who shows mercy.

—Romans 9:14-16, NABRE

CHAPTER FORTY-THREE
AMBASSADOR

LARRY'S STORY:

As a Christian, I am an Ambassador of God's love, grace, and mercy. An ambassador is someone who represents a nation or another person. I feel like I am an ambassador for Jesus Christ. That is, God is appealing to people through me, not just in my ministry as an ordained deacon, but through my ministry and my participation, and the common priesthood of Jesus Christ.

No, it is not easy to fulfill that job, because you are on the job 24/7. I am always a deacon, and more importantly, I am always a person that represents Christ. Yes, I guess this is the job that I have been searching for all of my life. I am privileged; this is the greatest work that a person can do, in my opinion. This is the greatest job that one can have!

Some people think that being a Christian is boring, but really, it is a great work because we know that there is the potentiality for eternal life in the presence of God. I don't think that's just a fairy tale. I believe that if we are faithful, Jesus will bring us to the house of the Father in the Parousia, at the end of time. I believe with all my heart that the Lord will come again in glory.

Matthew 24:36 teaches us that no man knows when the Lord will return. "But of that day and hour no one knows, neither the angels of heaven, nor the Son, but the Father alone." (NABRE) First Thessalonians 4:16-17 complete the picture of how that return might look:

> For the Lord himself, with a word of command, with the voice of an archangel and with the trumpet of God, will come down from heaven, and the dead in Christ will rise first. Then we who are alive, who are left, will be caught up together with them in the clouds to meet the Lord in the air. (NABRE)

I really believe that He will come again and I want to be in that number when He comes. I hold dear the knowledge that I have been given the privilege to minister the Gospel. I treasure this great responsibility. I know that with God and the power of His Holy Spirit that was given to me at baptism, and a fresh outpouring of it in confirmation, that I can do it. I believe that there is one baptism, but there are many fillings. In other words, God can fill us repeatedly to overflowing with His Holy Spirit. I am dependent upon that to execute my charge as a minister of the Gospel, and as a Christian.

The Cathedral is a beautiful place. It is the mother Church of the Archdiocese. The seat of the Archbishop is there at the Cathedral. The original cathedral was completed around 1726, but was one of the buildings burned to the ground in 1788. Construction of a new church began five years later and was completed in December 1794 making the Cathedral-Basilica of St. Louis King of France the oldest active cathedral still in service in the United States. I am privileged to be able to preach and minister at the Cathedral as a deacon.

Everything is very orderly there. After Mass we go out front to greet the people. People are always saying how much they enjoy the mass. My brother deacons with whom I serve with understand liturgy, and it is good liturgy. In other words, we give care to worshipping the Living God with dignity and reverence and honor. It is a wonderful blessing to me.

I am awed and overwhelmed with God's mercy and His grace, because I was a sinner, and I still am. I did not know that I was a sinner in the past. God's grace invaded my sinfulness. Romans 6:23 says, "For the wages of sin is death," yet, we live because of God's grace and His mercy.

"The Hound of Heaven" is what God is sometimes called; He is always looking for us. He is always looking! His sovereign act of looking for us is an act of His grace. In other words, He invades our space. We can reject the grace that God offers. Nevertheless, He invades our space and comes into our lives. He is always knocking at the door of our hearts.

Like the telephone commercial, God is always asking, "Can you hear me now? Can you hear me now?" He does that through people. He does that through circumstances. He did it for me. He actually used race and racism in reverse to bring me to His own bosom. How awesome is this God of ours?

Yes, because God has invaded me with His grace, He invites me to look at everybody the way that He does. I am not always perfect with that but He desires that I would look at everyone the way that He does. He says, *these are My created ones, I fashioned them with My own hands. I blew My breath into them. One may look different. One may have a better tan, or a little less tan, but they are all Mine. My breath is in all of them.*

You should not be a racist, or be prejudiced and be a child of God. It is simply incongruent; those things cannot match up together. I struggled to ask God to forgive me about my past. His love requited my sinful past. According to Hebrews 9:22, "without the shedding of blood there is no forgiveness." (NABRE) Because God is omnipotent, omniscient, omnipresent, and all loving, God's own Son became the sacrifice. Therefore, instead of seeing my sin at the altar or in my life, He sees the blood of the Lamb, His Son, Jesus Christ.

I feel similar to how John Newton must have felt. (Newton was the Captain of a slave ship in the 1700s and he brought slaves from the coast of Africa, to England. One day, there was a great storm upon the sea. John Newton's ship was filled and the bowels of his ship were filled with black souls, with black African slaves. He was involved in the slave trade, a despicable business. However, it was a prestigious business, so he continued with it. One day a storm came upon the sea and John Newton was sure that not only his ship, but his cargo and his life would be lost. The storm raged, and the ship was tossed to and fro. The ship was saved, and his cargo was delivered safely.)

Later, meditating upon that great storm upon the sea, and the storm that had come up in his life, John Newton came up with a great song that every Christian knows. That song is "Amazing Grace." The words continue, "How sweet the sound, that saved a wretch like me. I once was lost, but now I'm found. I was blind, but now I see."

I was lost, just like John Newton. I was stuck in the slavery, if you will, the trade of misery and hatred, and God delivered me. I was blind; I could only see through the eyes of hatred, and through the eyes of race. All of a sudden, God's grace overwhelmed me, caught me, and removed the scales from my eyes. Then I could see in a new way, and now I do see in a new way. That is why I can say, like John Newton, "Amazing grace, how sweet the sound, that saved a wretch like me. I once was lost, but now I'm found. I was blind, but now I see." It feels good to be found.

I am still searching for more of God's grace and more of His light. I know that I am dependent upon God's mercy and His continual forgiveness. I know that I have been forgiven, I am being forgiven, and I will be forgiven.

As it is said in Revelation 12:11 (NABRE):

"They conquered him [the Devil] by the blood of the Lamb

and by the word of their testimony;

love for life did not deter them from death."

And what do we testify? It is this: that Christ has died. Christ has risen. And Christ will come again. That is our testimony.

John Newton's story resonated in me. That whole picture of the idea of hopeless black souls in the belly of the ship was just like having no hope on the plantation. The number of slaves, black souls in the belly of the ship, was greater than the number of the white captors on the deck of the ship. The crew was few in numbers, yet they controlled large numbers of black people with guns and chains.

Even though God's amazing grace has helped me overcome race, we still have a deep divide in race relations, not only in New Orleans but in our nation. I do not want any of my black brothers or sisters to think that I am naive because through God's mercy I have begun to overcome the power of race in my life—I no longer see color before person. I understand that it is still an issue in our city and our nation. I know it is still a problem; but I am praying about it. I refuse to be a victim of it because I believe that God's love is greater than race, because He has let me experience His overwhelming grace to help me to overcome the power of race.

God has shown me His amazing grace; not only to help overcome race, but by showing me that His Son, Jesus Christ, is His gift to the world and His personal gift to me as well.

"Blessed those who keep his testimonies,

who seek him with all their heart.

They do no wrong;

they walk in his ways."

— Psalm 119:2-3, NABRE

GOD'S GRACE:

We should go to God in prayer for all things. Here is a prayer composed by Archbishop Gregory Aymond of New Orleans for the people of New Orleans to overcome violence, murder, and racism:

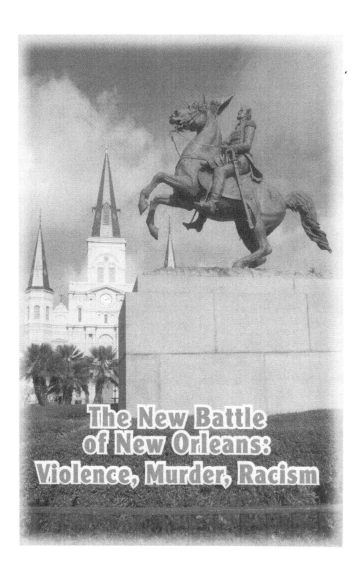

The New Battle of New Orleans: Violence, Murder, Racism

Loving and faithful God, through the years the people of our archdiocese have appreciated the prayers and love of Our Lady of Prompt Succor in times of war, disaster, epidemic and illness. We come to you, Father, with Mary our Mother, and ask you to help us in the battle of today against violence, murder and racism.

We implore you to give us your wisdom that we may build a community founded on the values of Jesus, which gives respect to the life and dignity of all people.

Bless parents that they may form their children in faith. Bless and protect our youth that they may be peacemakers of our time. Give consolation to those who have lost loved ones through violence.

Hear our prayer and give us the perseverance to be a voice for life and human dignity in our community.

We ask this through Christ our Lord. Amen.

Our Lady of Prompt Succor, hasten to help us.

Mother Henriette Delille, pray for us that we may be a holy family.

Dear Reader,

In writing this book, I have experienced many emotions. Looking back over my life and my journey toward a deeper relationship with God has reminded me of the struggles and triumphs, the heartache and God's healing in my life. *Amazing Grace Overcoming Race* is the beginning of a new phase of my ministry. I have begun writing my second book—*The Word, The Blood, and The Name* (of Jesus).

As my ministry grows and I continue to travel all over the United States teaching about God's love and grace, I ask for your intercession. Please know that I am praying that you will experience God's amazing grace in your life!

Faithfully yours,

Deacon Larry Oney

ABOUT THE AUTHOR

Deacon Larry D. Oney is a Permanent Deacon for the Diocese of New Orleans, Louisiana. He is assigned to Saint Louis King of France Cathedral in the historic French Quarter in New Orleans. He and his wife and their children reside in LaPlace, Louisiana and are members of Our Lady of Grace Catholic Church. Larry is the Chairman of the Board of HGI, Hammerman & Gainer International, and an active member of the New Orleans Chapter of Legatus. He is the chairman of the Board of Regents for Our Lady of Holy Cross College. Deacon Larry ministers nationally and internationally and has appeared on EWTN, Franciscan Radio, and Ava Maria Radio. Deacon Larry has a dynamic ministry of preaching, teaching, and exhortation. He utilizes humor, Sacred Scripture, and his love of the people of God, to speak to the heart of God's people in an uplifting manner.

1271687R00107

Made in the USA
San Bernardino, CA
06 December 2012